J. George Hodgins

The Law and Regulations

relating to public school trustees in rural sections, and to public school teachers and other school officers : with extracts from the municipal, assessment, and other statutes relating to the same

J. George Hodgins

The Law and Regulations
relating to public school trustees in rural sections, and to public school teachers and other school officers ; with extracts from the municipal, assessment, and other statutes relating to the same

ISBN/EAN: 9783337373566

Printed in Europe, USA, Canada, Australia, Japan

Cover: Foto ©Paul-Georg Meister /pixelio.de

More available books at **www.hansebooks.com**

REVISED SCHOOL LAW OF 1885.

THE

LAW AND REGULATIONS

RELATING TO

PUBLIC SCHOOL TRUSTEES

IN

RURAL SECTIONS,

AND TO

PUBLIC SCHOOL TEACHERS

AND OTHER SCHOOL OFFICERS.

WITH EXTRACTS FROM THE MUNICIPAL, ASSESSMENT, AND OTHER STATUTES RELATING TO THE SAME.

ALSO DECISIONS OF THE SUPERIOR COURTS THEREON,

DOWN TO THE PRESENT YEAR.

BY

J. GEORGE HODGINS, M.A., LL.D.,

BARRISTER-AT-LAW,

Deputy Minister of Education for Ontario.

TORONTO:
COPP, CLARK CO., 9 FRONT STREET WEST.
1885.

Entered according to Act of the Parliament of Canada, in the year one thousand eight hundred and eighty-five, by JOHN GEORGE HODGINS, LL.D., Barrister-at-Law, in the Office of the Minister of Agriculture.

CONTENTS.

	PAGE
LIST OF CASES DECIDED BY THE HIGH COURT OF JUSTICE	v
PREFATORY NOTE.—Preliminary Remarks in Regard to the Office of Trustee	5
CHAPTER I.—The Office of Trustee	6
CHAPTER II.—Powers and Duties of Trustees	14
CHAPTER III.—Duties of a Secretary-Treasurer and Collector	24
CHAPTER IV.—The Law Relating to Non-Residents	31
CHAPTER V.—School Section Auditors—Accountability of Trustees	33
CHAPTER VI.—Public School Meetings	38
CHAPTER VII.—Selection of School Sites	54
CHAPTER VIII.—Compulsory Attendance of Absentee Children	54
CHAPTER IX.—Public School Teachers	56
CHAPTER X.—Superannuation of School Teachers	67
CHAPTER XI.—Relation of Inspectors to Public School Teachers	69
CHAPTER XII.—Schools in Unorganized Townships	72
CHAPTER XIII.—General Provisions of the Law, Applicable to all Schools	78
CHAPTER XIV.—School Terms, Holidays and Vacations	81
CHAPTER XV.—County Model Schools	81
CHAPTER XVI.—Teachers' Institutes	82
CHAPTER XVII.—Teachers' Associations	82
ANALYTICAL INDEX	85

LIST OF EIGHTY-SEVEN CASES

AFFECTING

PUBLIC SCHOOLS,

DECIDED BY THE HIGH COURT OF JUSTICE, ONTARIO, SINCE 1850,
AND QUOTED IN THIS WORK.

	PAGE.
Anderson v. Vansittart, 5 Q. B. 335	63
Anglin v. Minis, 18 C. P. 170	78
Applegarth v. Graham, 7 C. P. 171	77
Berlin v. Grange, 5 C. P. 211, and 1 E. & A. 279	78
Board of Education, *In re*, and Napanee, 29 Chy. 395	30
Birmingham v. Hungerford, 19 C. P. 411	65
Chief Superintendent, *In re* Kelly v. Hedges, 12 Q. B. 531	19
Chief Superintendent, *In re* McLean v. Farrell, 21 Q. B. 441	76
Chief Superintendent, *In re* Hogg v. Rogers, 15 C. P. 417	76
Chief Superintendent, *In re* Stark v. Montague, 14 Q. B. 473 ... 3,	77
Chief Superintendent, *In re* Milne v. Sylvester, 18 Q. B. 538	64
Coleman v. Kerr, 27 Q. B. 5	78
Craig v. Rankin, 10 C. P. 186	76
Croupland v. Nottawasaga, 15 Chy. 339	54
Denison v. Henry, 17 Q. B. 276	77
Dunwich, Trustees of, v. McBeatty, 4 C. P. 228	15
Dunn v. School Board of Windsor, 3 C. L. T. 551	21
Farris v. Irwin, 10 C. P. 116	12
Fetterly v. Russell, 14 Q. B. 433	9
Forbes v. Trustees, 8 C. P. 73, 74 .... 9, 15,	20
Fraser v. Page, 18 Q. B. 336	77
Ferris v. Chesterfield, 10 C. P. 272, 6 L. J. 272	26
Foster v. Stokes, 2 O. R. 590	44
Gillies v. Wood, 13 Q. B. 357	77
Glen v. Grand Trunk Railway, 2 P. R. 377	48

LIST OF CASES CITED.

	PAGE.
Graham v. Hungerford, 29 Q. B. 239	14
*Grantham v. Toronto, 2 Q. B. 475	77
Holcolm v. Shaw, 22 Q. B. 92	78
Hughes v. Pake et al., 25 Q. B. 95	11
Hamilton, Trustees of, v. Neil, 28 Chy. 408	25, 65
Jarvis v. Cayley, 11 Q. B. 282	78
Johnson v. Trustees, 30 Q. B. 264	20
Joice, In re Lawrence, 19 Q. B. 197	64
Keith v. Fenelon Falls, 3 O. R. 194	25
Kennedy v. Burness, 15 Q. B. 473	11
Kennedy v. Hall, 7 C. P. 218	12
Kennedy v. Sandwich, 9 Q. B. 326	31
Lambiere v. Trustees South Cayuga, 7 A. R. 506	65
Lamont v. Trustees Aldboro', 5 U. C. L. J. 93	13
Lee v. Public School Board Toronto, 32 C. P. 78	13
McBride v. Gardham, 8 C. P. 296	78
McCormick, In re, and Corporation Colchester South, 1 C. L. T. 215	
McIntyre v. McBean, 13 Q. B. 534	64
McMillan v. Rankin, 19 Q. B. 356	76
Marshall v. Trustees, 4 C. P. 373	19
Martin v. Kergan, 2 Pr. R. 370	48
Monaghan v. Ferguson, 3 Q. B. 484	20
Munson, In re, v. Collingwood, 9 C. P. 479	15
Morrison v. Arthur, 13 Q. B. 297	54
Ness v. Saltfleet, 13 Q. B. 408	54
Newberry v. Stephens, 16 Q. B. 65	76
Orr v. Ranney, 12 Q. B. 377	9, 15, 51
Oakland v. Proper, 1 O. R. 330	30
O'Leary, In re, and Blandford, 19 Q. B. 556	31
O'Donohoe v. School Trustees, Thorah, 5 C. P. 297	64
Quin v. Trustees, 7 Q. B. 130	63, 64
Rabrais v. Trustees, 12 Chy. 115	20
Ranney v. Maclem, 9 C. P. 192	12
Regina v. Trustees Tyendinaga, 20 Q. B. 528	11
Regina v. Trustees, 3 P. R. 43	13
Regina, Ex rel., Stewart v. Standish, 4 C. L. T. 392	13

LIST OF CASES CITED.

	PAGE.
Ridsdale v. Brush, 22 Q. B. 122	77
Ryland v. King, 12 C. P. 198	52
School Trustees of Hamilton v. Neil, 28 Chy. 408	25, 30
School Trustees v. Hunter, 10 C. P. 359	75
School Trustees, *In re*, v. Casement, 17 Q. B. 275	77
School Trustees v. Caledon, 12 C. P. 301	160
School Trustees v. Farrell, 27 Q. B. 321, 5 L. J. 230	53
Scott v. Trustees, 21 C. P. 398	20
Scott v. Trustees, 19 Q. B. 28	20
Secretary of War v. Toronto, 22 Q. B. 551	78
Smith v. Belleville, 16 Chy. 130	54
Spry v. Mumby, 11 C. P. 285	15, 16, 76
Spry v. McKenzie, 18 Q. B. 161	75
Squire v. Mooney, 30 Q. B. 531	78
Stephen, Trustees of, v. Mitchell, 29 Q. B. 382	25
Tiernan v. Nepean, 15 Q. B. 87	77
Toronto v. McBride, 29 Q. B. 13	12
Trustees No. 2 Dunwich v. McBeatty, 4 C. P. 228	15
Trustees v. Mitchell, 29 Q. B. 382	25
Vanburen v. Bull, 19 Q. B. 633	12
Vance v. King, 21 Q. B. 187	48, 51, 52
Walsh v. Leahy, 18 C. P. 48	64
Williams v. Trustees, 7 C. P. 559	51
Wilson v. Thompson, 9 C. P. 364	13
Wyoming v. Bell, 24 Chy. 564	53
Wright v. Trustees of Stephen, 32 Q. B. 541	64

PUBLIC SCHOOL LAW

RELATING TO

TRUSTEES IN RURAL SECTIONS.

PASSED IN 1885.

PRELIMINARY REMARKS IN REGARD TO THE OFFICE OF TRUSTEE.

NOTE.—There are certain equitable principles which apply to the trustees and their office, (some of which do not arise under the School Law,) to which it is proper to refer in this place, as follows :—

1.—A Trustee defined.

A trustee may be regarded as a person to whom money, or other property or valuables, is intrusted to expend or manage, under certain rules or directions, for the use or benefit of another party.

2.—What a Trustee is expected to do.

In the discharge of his duties, a trustee is required to use the customary care and diligence usually exercised by a man of ordinary prudence and vigilance in the management of his own affairs.

3.—Responsibilities of a Trustee.

A trustee is responsible :—

(*a*) For his own acts, and for the acts of his colleagues done with his knowledge.

(*b*) For all breaches of trust, or default committed by himself, or by his colleagues, to which he is privy, or in which he expressly or tacitly acquiesces, or which would not have happened but for his own negligence, act or default.

(*c*) (*Under the School Law*) a trustee is personally responsible for neglect of duty; refusal to act when lawfully required to do so; neglect to take security from secretary-treasurer; or for loss of school money through his wilful act, negligence or carelessness in not keeping the school open; in not reporting to Inspector, and in not compelling the attendance of absentees. (School Act, secs. 221, 257, 258, 260, 261 and 271.)

(*d*) (*Under the School Law*) trustees are responsible should they pay "compensation money or any part thereof," for a school site to a party not entitled to receive the same—saving always their recourse against such party. (*Ibid.* sec. 79.)

4.—What a Trustee may do.

He may, with the consent of his colleagues:

(*a*) Defray out of the trust fund expenses legitimately and properly incurred.

(*b*—*Under the School Law*)—Receive remuneration as collector of school rates.

(*c*—*Under the School Law*)—Receive payment for a school site.

5.—What a Trustee may not do.

Unless allowed by Statute, or other authoritative direction, a trustee cannot lawfully:

(*a*) Receive, even with the consent of his colleagues, any salary or remuneration for his services in the capacity of trustee.

(*b*) Make any personal profit out of the trust.

(*c*) Mix up trust money or accounts with his own private money or accounts.

(*d*—*Under the School Law*)—Enter into a contract with, or have a pecuniary claim (except in the two instances mentioned above) on the corporation of which he is a member. (See School Act, sec. 253.)

(*e*—*Ibid.*)—Act as bookseller's agent, or sell books, maps, apparatus or other requisites to the school. (See School Act, sec. 272.)

CHAPTER I.

THE OFFICE OF TRUSTEE.

Section 1.—Who may be a Public School Trustee.

Any "actual resident ratepayer" in a public school section, "and of the full age of twenty-one years, and not disqualified under this Act," may be elected a trustee of such section. (School Act, sec. 13. See (*h*) of this chapter, next page.)

2.—Who may not be a Public School Trustee.

The law excludes the following persons from the office of school trustee :

(a) A non-resident of the section, or school division. (School Act, sections 13 and 252.)
(b) A resident, who is not an assessed ratepayer. (*Ibid.*)
(c) An inspector of public schools. (Sec. 251.)
(d) A teacher in a high, public or separate school. (*Ibid.*)
(e) Minors under twenty-one years of age. (*Ibid.* sec. 13.)

3.—The Office of School Trustee may be vacated as follows:

(a) *By refusal to act*, and payment of *five* dollars as a penalty for such refusal, immediately after election to office. (*Ibid.* sec. 256.)

(b) *By resignation*, with the consent in writing of his colleagues. (*Ibid.* sec. 25.)

(c) *Neglect to make Verbal Declaration.*—On being fined five dollars by a magistrate for neglect, or refusal, to make a verbal declaration of office before the chairman of the school meeting or a magistrate (or before the secretary of the meeting should the chairman be elected trustee), before entering on his duties. (*Ibid.* secs. 23 and 250.)

(d) *Neglect of Duty.*—On being fined *twenty* dollars for neglecting or refusing to perform the duties of his office—not having, on his election (as in (a) above), refused to accept office, and having paid the prescribed penalty of *five* dollars for such refusal. (*Ibid.* sec. 257.)

(e) *Removal.*—By actual removal of domicile from the section.

(f) *Non-Residence.*—By three consecutive months' absence from the meetings of the school corporation without being authorized by resolution entered upon the trustees' minute book. (*Ibid.* sec. 252.)

(g) *Outside the Boundaries.*—On being placed outside of the section boundaries, by reason of an alteration in them. (See note to section 6 of this chapter.)

(h) *Conviction* for any felony or misdemeanor, or becoming insane. (*Ibid.* sec. 252.)

4.—Verbal Declaration of Office required to be made.

Within two weeks after his election, the new trustee is required to make the following verbal declaration of office, in presence of the chairman of the school meeting:—

"I will truly and faithfully, to the best of my judgment and ability, discharge the duties of the office of school trustee, to which I have been elected." (School Act, secs. 23 and 250.)

NOTE.—If the chairman himself be elected trustee, he should make the declaration of office before a magistrate, or the secretary of the school meeting. In the case of neglect or refusal to do so—in either case—the trustee-elect subjects himself to a fine of *twenty* dollars, to be recovered before a magistrate, for the benefit of the section. Immediately on the imposition of this fine, the office is vacated, and a new election should be held; but, in the meantime, the *bona fide* acts of the trustee who was fined, if he should perform any, are binding upon the section. (See section 3, and note to section 6 of this chapter.)

5.—Trustee's Three Years' Term of Office.

Every trustee holds office for three years, and until his successor is elected. This rule does not apply to the second and third trustees elected at a *first* school meeting in a section. One of these trustees (the second elected) holds office for two years, and the other (the third elected) holds it for one year, and in all cases until their respective successors are appointed. (*Ibid.* sec. 30.)

NOTE.—After serving his full term, a person cannot be compelled to act again as trustee until after the expiration of four years; but he may, with his own consent, be re-elected on his going out of office. This privilege does not extend to a person who declines to act as trustee, and pays the fine of *five* dollars for non-service. Such a person may be elected to fill the next succeeding vacancy, but may again decline to serve, on payment of *five* dollars, as before. (*Ibid.* secs. 26 and 256.)

6.—Who are the Trustees of altered School Sections.

That part of a divided or altered section, in which the school house of the section continues to be situated, is held to be the old or original section. The trustees who live in this old part remain the lawful trustees of the section, and only go out of office on the expiration of their term of service. Those only who, by the alteration of the section, are placed outside of the new boundaries—and thus become non-residents—cease to be trustees when the alteration takes effect (25th of December). (See (*g*) of sec. 3, page 7, also "Note" below.)

NOTE.—As a general rule, it is scarcely worth while to anticipate the annual meeting, and elect a trustee or trustees in place of the one (or two) who may cease to hold office on the 25th December, by reason of non-residence, caused by being placed outside the new boundaries, as explained above. The remaining trustee or trustees in the section (as well as the secretary or inspector) can give notice of the annual school meeting. Should, however, an election be held before the annual meeting, another election must be held at the annual meeting, on the first Wednesday in December, to fill up the usual vacancy caused by the retiring trustee.

7.—Liability of the original section for old debts.

The Court of Common Pleas has decided that one or more alterations in the boundaries of a school section, or the change of ownership of land in the section by many of the ratepayers originally liable, did not relieve the trustees of the responsibility of paying a just debt due by the original section before any such alteration was made. (See decision (4), section 13, of chapter ii.) This general principle was also incorporated in the School Law of 1885, sec. 136, so far as loans made to the trustees of any section is concerned. The land in such section at the time when the loan is effected continues liable for the debt until repaid, even should it in the meantime be placed outside of the boundaries of the school section, by reason of their alteration.

8.—Power of the Retiring Trustee at the Close of his Term.

The restriction on the power of the "retiring trustee," at the close of his term of office, having been removed by the School Act, he has now equal power and authority with either of his colleagues to perform all lawful acts up to the day of his leaving office.

9.—Personal Liability of Trustees—How it arises.

The personal responsibility of trustees arises in various ways, (under the School Act and Regulations), among others, as follows:

(*a*) For neglect to keep open a school during the whole school year, to send in reports to the inspector, or to compel the attendance of absentees under the compulsory clauses of the statute, and the consequent loss of any part of the school fund to the section. (See School Act, secs. 221, 268 and 271, and (*j*) of this sec.)

(*b*) For any loss incurred, in consequence of neglect to take security from their secretary-treasurer, collector, or other person entrusted with school moneys. (School Act, sec. 261.)

NOTE.—This security should be lodged with the clerk of the township council. (*Ibid*, sec. 33.)

(*c*) Neglect to transact trustee business, at trustee meetings duly called (of which each trustee must have due notice). (*Ibid*, sec. 36.)

NOTE.—Trustees are, of course, free to converse at pleasure with each other, and informally to agree on any school business; but all official acts must be agreed to at a meeting to which all the trustees are summoned. (See NOTE to clause (5) section 1, chapter iii.)

Thus, if a verbal contract or agreement, without the knowledge of the other trustee, be made by two trustees with other parties acting in good faith, such agreement or understanding would necessarily bind the corporation, and not the individual trustees who entered into it, and it can be enforced against the corporation. Thus a contract signed by two trustees, and sealed with the corporate seal, can be enforced against the corporation. This rule also applies to minor purchases and unimportant orders for work required to be done for the corporation, and involving an outlay. (See *Fetterly* v. *Russell & Cambridge* (on simple contract debts), 14 Q. B. R. 433.) In such cases trustees should authorize one of themselves, or their secretary, to attend to such matters on their behalf. No trustee (as we have shown) can enter into a contract with the corporation of which he is a member, or have any pecuniary claim on it, except for a school site, or as collector of school rates, when duly appointed by his colleagues. No act of the school corporation requires the assent, or necessarily the presence, of each individual trustee. It is sufficient that each of the three trustees have been individually notified of the trustee meeting, and that a majority of the three trustees thus notified concurs in the act itself. The following decisions of the Superior Courts sustain this view:—

(1.) *Two School Trustees can enter into a Contract against the wishes of a third.*—The Court of Common Pleas has decided that a contract entered into by two trustees under the School Acts, with the corporate seal attached, is sufficient; and a plea that it was signed by the two subscribing trustees without the consent or approbation of the third, was *held* to be bad.—*Forbes* v. *Trustees No. 8, Plympton*, 8 C. P. R. 74.

(2.) *But two Trustees cannot act without consulting a third.*—The Court of

Queen's Bench has decided that two of the trustees of a school are not competent to act in all cases without consulting a third, and giving him an opportunity of uniting in or opposing the acts of his colleagues.—*Orr* v. *Ranney et al., No. 15, Westminster.* 12 Q. B. R. 377.

(See other decisions of the courts, in section 13, chapter ii.)

(*d*) *For wilful neglect* or refusal "to exercise all the corporate "powers vested in them * * * for the fulfilment of any contract or "agreement made by them." (School Act, sec. 258. See also decisions in sec. 10 of this chap., and note to cl. (3) sec. 3 of chap. viii.)

(*e*) *Declaration of Office—Duty.*—For refusal or neglect to make the declaration of office, or to perform their lawful duties after having accepted office, a fine of *five* or *twenty* dollars (as the case may be) may be enforced by a magistrate. (See School Act, secs. 250 and 257, sec. 4 of this chapter, page 7.)

(*f*) *Notes of Hand.*—For all notes of hand which they may sign (not authorized by law.) The School Act, sec. 40, cl. (4.), authorizes trustees to give notes of hand for money to pay teachers' salaries.

NOTE.—The signature of two or more trustees to notes of hand, and even the affixing to them of the corporate seal, do not necessarily relieve individual trustees of personal responsibility in regard to them, or give to such notes a corporate character, unless they are given for loans raised with which to pay the teacher's salary. In that case they may be given, bearing not more than eight per cent. (See (*f*) above. The law, however, gives trustees ample powers at all times to procure by rate, imposed by the township council, such money as they may require. Trustees who desire to borrow money for the purchase of a site and the erection of a school house, can do so from the municipal council; as provided by the 381st sec. of the Consolidated Municipal Act of 1883, 46 Vic., ch. 18). This section authorizes "any municipal corporation having surplus moneys set apart for educational purposes, by by-law, to invest the same in a loan or loans to any board or boards of school trustees within the limits of the municipality, for such term or terms, and at such rate or rates of interest as may be agreed upon by and between the parties to such loan or loans respectively, and set forth in such by-law, or may by by-law grant any portion of such moneys or other general funds by way of gift to aid poor school sections within the municipality." (See decisions of the Courts, section 3, chapter ii.)

(*g*) *Unqualified Teachers.*—For the salary of teachers, or assistants (employed by them), who do not possess legal certificates of qualification during the whole period of their engagement. (See chapter ix.)

(*h*) *Refusal to account.*—For their own refusal, or that of their secretary (on their behalf), to furnish either of the school section auditors with the papers or information in their possession, or within their jurisdiction, relative to their school accounts. (See chapter v.)

(*i*) *Account for Moneys.*—For neglect or refusal to account to competent authority for school moneys or other school property entrusted to them, or in their possession. (See chapter v.)

(*j*) *Neglect of Law and Regulations.*—For loss to the section, of any portion of the legislative grant (or county assessment), in consequence of their neglect or refusal to keep their school open during the entire year, or of neglect to make reports and returns to the inspector, or of their refusal to conduct their school according to law or to the official regulations (which have the force of law.)

(k) Further Monetary Penalties for Neglect of Duty :

(1.) *Twenty* dollars for making a false return to the Inspector.

(2.) *Five* dollars for every week of delay in forwarding their annual report to the Inspector. (School Act, sections 269 and 270.)

(3.) *Five* dollars for neglect, in not calling annual or other necessary school meetings. (*Ibid* 254.)

10.—Legal Decisions on the Personal Liability of Trustees.

(1.) *Personal Liability or neglect or refusal to exercise their Corporate powers.*—The Court of Queen's Bench has decided as follows :—In a case where a mandamus *nisi* was issued to school trustees to levy the amount of a judgment obtained against them, no return was made, and a rule *nisi* for an attachment issued. In answer to this rule, one trustee swore that he always had been and still was desirous to obey the writ, and had repeatedly asked the others to join with him in levying the rate, but that they had refused. Another swore that owing to ill-health, with the consent of his co-trustees and the local superintendent, he had resigned his office before the writ was granted. The court, under these circumstances, discharged the rule *nisi* as against these two, on payment of costs of the application, and granted an attachment against the other trustee, who had taken no notice either of the mandamus or rule.—*Regina* v. *Trustees of School Section No. 27, Tyendinaga.* 20 Q. B. R. 528.

(2.) The Court of Queen's Bench has decided that, as by the [*sixteenth*] clause of the [*twelfth*] section of 13. and 14 Vic. c. 48 (similar to the Consolidated School Act, section 27, sub-section 20), the trustees can only be personally liable when they have wilfully neglected or refused to exercise their corporate powers; such neglect or refusal should have been alleged and shown in the award, to warrant its directions to levy on the trustees personally.—*Kennedy* v. *Burness et al, No. 5, Oneida.* 15 Q. B. R. 473.

Held, following *Kennedy* v. *Burness,* 15 Q. B. 487, that arbitrators between school trustees and a teacher, under the Common School Act, acting within their jurisdiction, are entitled to protection under S. C. U. C., c. 126, as persons fulfilling a public duty; and therefore that trespass would not be against them and their bailiff for seizing goods to enforce their award under sec. 86. It was contended that the arbitrator has no jurisdiction, as no contract under the corporate seal required by 23 Vict., c. 49, s. 12, was proved to have been produced before them; but the plaintiff's witness said an agreement was produced which he thought had the seal, and the plaintiff, as a trustee, had named an arbitrator and submitted the matters in dispute. *Held,* that under these circumstances it might be assumed that the arbitrators had before them all that was necessary to give jurisdiction. *Held,* also, that the award set out in the case was sufficient; and that the Act, 23 Vict., c. 49, s 9, which directs that no want of form shall invalidate such awards, should receive a liberal construction.—*Hughes* v. *Pake, et al.,* 25 Q. B., 95.

(3.) *Neglect of Trustees to exercise their Corporate Powers must be proved.*—The Court of Common Pleas also decided another similar case as follows:—In an action of replevin for goods of school trustees distrained under an award for the salary of a school teacher, declaring the trustees individually liable on the ground " that the trustees did not exercise all the corporate powers vested in them by the

School Acts for the due fulfilment of the contract" made by them with such teacher. *Held*, that the award as evidence, did not support pleas which averred as required by the [*sixteenth*] clause of the [*twelfth*] section of 13 and 14 Vic. c. 48 (similar to the Consolidated School Act, section 27, sub-section 20), a wilful neglect or refusal by the trustees to exercise their corporate powers as the ground for making them personally liable. 2. That on the facts, the defendants as trustees were not personally liable, the award ascertaining for the first time the exact amount due to the teacher, and declaring the trustees personally liable without giving them any opportunity to exercise their corporate powers to raise the money to pay it.—*Kennedy* v. *Hall et al, No. 5, Oneida*. 7 C. P. R. 218.

NOTE.—An award for a teacher's salary cannot now be made. All salary disputes between trustees and teachers must be settled in the Division Courts. (School Act, sec. 160.)

(4.) The same Court has decided that where trustees become personally liable under the statute, it is necessary to show that there has been some adjudication of the fact of wilful neglect or refusal to exercise the corporate powers vested in them for the fulfilment of any contract or agreement made by them, before such liability can be enforced.—*Ranney* v. *Maclem et al*, 9 C. P. R. 192.

(5.) *When Personal Liability of Trustee arises.*—The Court of Queen's Bench has decided that trustees cannot be held liable unless they wilfully neglect to do their duty: not where they decline in good faith to exercise their corporate powers on account of any doubt or legal difficulty which they suppose to exist.—*Vanburen* v. *Bull et al, No. 2, Rawdon*. 19 Q. B. R. 633.

NOTE.—See also *Tp. Toronto* v. *McBride's*, No. ( ) of sec. , chap. .

(6.) *A Trustee (not being secretary-treasurer) cannot receive School Moneys.*—The Court of Common Pleas has decided that a school trustee having money in his hands, not as secretary and treasurer of a board, or in any official capacity, cannot embezzle such money, his duty as trustee not requiring or authorizing him to receive it.—*Farris* v. *Irwin*, No. 16 Darlington, 10 C. P. R. 116.

(7.) *Loan to School Trustees—Personal Liability—Change of School Site.*—Two of the trustees of a school section, wishing to change the school site, called a meeting of the freeholders and householders, who rejected the proposal. The two trustees thereupon chose an arbitrator, assuming to act under sec. 30 Consol. Stat. U. C. ch. 64, but none was chosen by the freeholders and householders, and under the advice of the Deputy Superintendent the trustees called another meeting, at which a motion to appoint such arbitrator was rejected. The trustees' arbitrator and the local superintendent thereupon made an award changing the site. A special meeting was then called to consider how the money should be raised to carry out the change, at which the conduct of the trustees and the change was strongly disapproved of. The two trustees thereupon petitioned the township council, stating that the ratepayers were desirous of purchasing a new site, and asking for a loan of $400, "for which the trustees will bind themselves to pay the interest annually, and the principal when due." This was granted, and secured by two instalments, as follows :—

"We, the undersigned, Trustees of School Section No. 11, do hereby promise to pay the Treasurer of the Corporation of Toronto Township, or," &c.

(Signed) M. D. } *Trustees.*

with the corporate seal affixed. The money was expended for the purpose mentioned. The township corporation having sued the trustees individually on these notes, and on the common counts: *Held*, that they could not recover on the notes, for, (1) They were payable to the treasurer; and (2) The defendants were not personally liable upon them. *Held*, also, *Wilson, J.* dissenting, the defendants were not liable upon the common counts either, for the intention of all parties plainly was that the trustees as a corporation should be bound, not the defendants personally; and there being no fraud and concealment on their part, the fact that they as a corporation had no authority to borrow, nor the plaintiffs to lend, could not, under the circumstances, make them personally liable. *Semble, per Richards, C. J.*, that under section 30, the difference of opinion as to the change of site authorized a reference to arbitration; but that the refusal of the freeholders and householders to name an arbitrator did not enable the other two arbitrators to proceed, the proper course being to compel the appointment by mandamus. *Per Wilson, J.*, the difference of opinion must be as to the position of the new site, after the change has been agreed to by the ratepayers, not as to whether there shall be a change; and the arbitration, therefore, was unauthorized.—*The Corporation of the Township of Toronto* v. *McBride et al., Executors of William McBride,* 29 Q. B. R, 13.

(8.) *Not obeying the Writ.*—It has been decided in Chambers, that "No attachment will lie for not making a return to a peremptory mandamus;" it should be for not obeying the writ. The rule *nisi* called upon the trustees of school section 27 in the township of Tyendinaga, in the County of Hastings, to shew cause why an attachment should not issue against them. On an affidavit of service of this rule on A, B and C, stating them to be trustees of said section, a rule absolute was granted, following it in form, and thereupon an attachment issued against A, B and C. *Held,* bad, as not warranted by the rule. *Queen* v. *27 Tyendenaga.* 3 P. R. 43, C. L. Chamb.—*Burns.*

(9.) *Public School Trustee—Contract—Disqualification—Costs*—Where a school trustee, who was a medical practitioner, acted in his professional capacity under an engagement by the board in examining the pupils attending the school as to the prevalence of infectious disease, and made a charge of $15 therefor, which the board ordered to be paid.

Held, that this disqualified him as such trustee and rendered his seat vacant.

A rule for leave to exhibit an information in the nature of a *quo warranto* to test the defendant's right to retain his seat was directed to be made absolute without costs, unless within ten days the defendant admitted he had forfeited his seat and consented to the board declaring it vacant, in which case the rule was to be discharged without costs.—*Regina ex rel. Stewart* v. *Standish,* C. L. J., iv., 392.

(10.) *Disqualification of Trustees—Furnishing School Supplies.* —*Held,* Osler, J., doubting, on a special case stated for the opinion of the Court of Chancery and transferred to this court, that the fact of the public school board of the city of Toronto entering into an agreement with and purchasing their stationery and school supplies from a publishing company, and having obtained gas from a gas company, and insured their properties in certain insurance companies, of which said companies the plaintiff was a shareholder, did not disqualify him from acting as a trustee of the school board, or render his seat vacant, under 44 Vict., c. 30, s. 10, O.—*Lee* v. *The Public School Board of the City of Toronto,* 32 C. P. 78.

Quære, per Osler, J., whether the case could properly be entertained, no fact being disclosed by which jurisdiction could be exercised under the Act relating to mandamus and injunction, R. S. O., c. 52, s. 30, no wrongful act having been actually done by the school board, but merely an injury to the plaintiff's rights threatened, it being alleged that the board intended to declare the seat vacant.—*Ibid.*

(11.) *Trustees cannot be Contractors or Builders—School Houses.*—A school trustee cannot, even by the consent of his co-trustees, be a contractor for the building of a school house.—*Lamont* v. *The School Trustees of Section No. 3, Aldboro,* 5 L. J. 93—D. C., Hughes.

Held, that power is given, under 13 and 14 Vict. c. 48, 16 Vict. c. 185, to school trustees to assemble a special meeting of the freeholders and householders of any school section for the purpose of maintaining a common school within their section:—*Held*, also, that any resolution passed at the general annual meeting may be rescinded by a special meeting properly convened for that purpose.—*Wilson* v. *Thompson*, 9 C. P.

(12.) *Personal Liability of Trustees—Refusing to Exercise Corporate Powers.*
School trustees cannot be held liable under 23 Vict. c. 49, s. 9, for wilfully neglecting or refusing to comply with an award, without being at first afforded an odportunity of explaining or justifying such non-compliance. Where, therefore, the defendant was justified seizing the plaintiffs goods under a warrant of the arbitrators issued against the plaintiff and the other trustees for non-complience with an award, but did not shew that the plaintiff was notified or called upon to shew cause before such warrant issued. *Held*, that the plea was bad. Remarks as to the informality of the warrant. *Graham* v. *Hungerford et al.* 29 Q. B. 239.

CHAPTER II.
POWERS AND DUTIES OF TRUSTEES.

I.—GENERAL CORPORATE POWERS.

1.—Rural School Trustees to be a Corporation.

The law declares that "the trustees in every school section shall be a corporation, under the name of *The Board of Public School Trustees for Section —— of the Township of ——, in the County of ——*. And no such corporation shall cease by reason of want of trustees. In case of such want (*a*) any two ratepayers of the section, or the Inspector, may, by giving *six* days' notice, * * * call a meeting of the assessed freeholders, householders or tenants who shall proceed to elect three trustees. * * * The trustees thus elected shall hold and retire from office, in the manner prescribed "in this Act." (School Act, secs. 27 and 33.)

2.—General Powers and Liabilities of a Corporation.

The Consolidated Interpretation Act, Ont. (1877), further declares that " Words making any association or number of persons a corporation, or body politic and corporate, shall vest in such corporation power to sue and be sued ; to contract and be contracted with in their corporate name ; to have a common seal,* and to alter or change the same at their pleasure; to have perpetual succession, and power to acquire and

---

* A corporation being an invisible body, cannot manifest its will by oral communication ; a peculiar mode has therefore been devised for the authentic expression of its intention—namely, the affixing of its common seal ; and it is held that though the particular members may express their private consent by words or signing their names, yet this does not bind the corporation ; it is the fixing of the seal, and that only, which unites the several assents of the individuals composing it, and makes one joint assent of the whole.—*Smith's Mercantile Law*, b. i, *chap*. 4.

hold personal property and movables for the purposes for which the corporation is constituted, and to alienate the same at pleasure ; and shall also vest in any majority of the members of the corporation, the power to bind the others by their acts; and shall exempt the individual members of the corporation from personal liability for its debts or obligations or acts, provided they do not contravene the provisions of the Act incorporating them. (Rev. Stat. Ont. ch. 1, cl. 24'. But no corporation shall carry on the business of banking [*i.e.* taking or issuing promissory notes, &c.,] unless when such power is expressly conferred on them by Statute. (See " *Decisions of Courts,*" next section (1).

3.—Legal Decisions regarding School Trustee Corporations.

(1.) *Circulation of School Orders on Treasurer, an Act of Banking contrary to Law.*—Chief Justice Draper thus condemns unauthorized acts of banking on the part of corporations. He says : " The evidence given at this trial shows that a practice had grown up for the defendants to give orders on their treasurer, which, when he had accepted them, got into circulation, and at last found their way into the collector's hands in payment of taxes. Such a practice seems to me at variance with the spirit, if not the intention, of the Consolidated Municipal Act, which enacts that no council shall act as a banker, or issue any bond, bill, note, debenture, or other undertaking of any kind, or in any form of the nature of a bank-bill or note, or intended to form a circulating medium, or to pass as money ; and any bond, bill, note, debenture, or other undertaking issued in contravention of this section, shall be void.—*In re Munson* v. *The Municipality of Collingwood,* 9 C. P. R. 497.

(2.) *A Corporation aggregate is not bound to appear as Witnesses in Court, but its Individual Members may be subpœnaed.*—The Court of Common Pleas has decided that a corporation aggregate is not bound to appear at the trial as witnesses, under a notice served on its attorney under the Consolidated Statute, chap. 32, sec. 15 (now R. S. O., chap. 62, sec. 18). If the individual members are required to appear, they must be individually subpœnaed.—*Trustees No. 2, Dunwich* v. *McBeath,* 4 C. P. R. 228.

(3.) *Two School Trustees can enter into a Contract against the wishes of a third.*—The Court of Common Pleas has decided that a contract entered into by two trustees under the School Acts, with the corporate seal attached, is sufficient, and a plea that it is signed by the two subscribing trustees without the consent or approbation of the third, [but not without his knowledge,] was *held* to be bad.—*Forbes* v. *Trustees, No. 8, Plympton.* 8 C. P. R. 74. (See next decision.)

(4.) *But two Trustees cannot Act without consulting a third.*—The Court of Queen's Bench has decided that two of the trustees of a school are not competent to act in all cases without consulting the third, and giving him an opportunity of uniting in or opposing the acts of his colleagues.—*Orr* v. *Ranney, et al., No. 15, Westminster.* 12 Q. B. R. 377.

(5.) *A Trustee, when sued for a Corporate Act, entitled to Notice of Action.*—The Court of Common Pleas has decided, in a case of alleged trespass under a warrant, that a school trustee who is sued for any act done in his corporate capacity, is entitled to notice of action, and that the action must be brought within six months ; and that a school trustee, acting in the discharge of his duty as such, is entitled to the protection of, and comes within the Consolidated Statutes, chap. 126 (now R. S. O., chap. 73), notwithstanding he should have signed a warrant individually, instead of in his corporate capacity.—*Spry* v. *Munby et al., No. 15 Rawdon.* 11 C. P. R. 285.

(6.) *Protection of Trustees, Collectors, and other lawful School Officers.*—The following are the provisions of the Act for the protection of magistrates and others, to which the judge in the foregoing decisions referred.

Sec. 1. Every action brought against any Justice of the Peace, for any act done by him in the execution of his duty as such Justice, with respect to any matter within his jurisdiction as said Justice, *or against any other officer or person fulfilling any public duty, for anything by him done in the performance of such public duty,* [interpreted by the court in the foregoing case (11 C. P. R. 285) to apply to school trustees and to collectors of school rates, when acting under the trustees' lawful warrant] whether any of such duties arise out of the common law or be imposed by Act of Parliament, either Imperial or Provincial, shall be an action on the case for a tort, and in the declaration it shall be expressly alleged that such act was done maliciously and without reasonable and probable cause ; and if at the trial of any such action, upon the general issue pleaded, the plaintiff fails to prove such allegation, he shall be nonsuited, or a verdict shall be given for defendant. * * * * * * * *

Sec. 20. So far as applicable, the whole of this Act shall apply for the protection of every officer and person mentioned in the first section hereof, for anything done in the execution of his office, as therein expressed.

NOTE.—The one hundred and fifty-fourth section of the Consolidated Public School Act o 1885, also provides that " Trustees shall not be liable to any prosecution, or the payment of any damages for acting under any by-law of a municipal council before it has been quashed."

II.—POWERS AND DUTIES OF TRUSTEES IN REGARD TO THE SITE AND SCHOOL HOUSE.

4.—Duty of Trustees in regard to the Site of a School House

A change of site can only take place by consent of a majority of the ratepayers present at a meeting called by the trustees (or the county inspector). Should a difference of opinion arise at the meeting between a majority of the trustees and the ratepayers on the choice of a new site, the matter must be referred to arbitration, as explained in the chapters relating to " School Meetings " and " School Sites ;" but the trustees alone have the legal right to decide upon the size or enlargement of a school site, as provided in sec. 10 of chap. vii.

5.—Trustees to hold School Property by any Title.

Trustees are required by law " To take possession and have the custody and safe keeping of all public school property which has been acquired or given for public school purposes in such section; to acquire and hold as a corporation, by any title whatsoever, any land, movable property, moneys, or income given or acquired at any time for public school purposes, and to hold or apply the same according to the terms on which the same were acquired or received." (School Act, sec. 40, cl. (9.) See also sec. 8 of this chapter, on next page.)

6.—Necessity for a proper Title to the School Site.

The provision of the law, and especially the one mentioned in section 8, below, which vests all school property in the trustee corporation for the purposes of sale, requires that trustees should, without delay, whenever practicable, obtain a deed,* a bond for a deed, a lease, or other legal instrument, granting to them quiet possession of the school site of their section, in case they have not a sufficient title to it.

(1.) Objection is frequently made to the right of trustees to assess the section for the building of, or repairs to, the school house, where no full legal title to the school premises is vested in them. To remove this objection (although it is only a technical one), trustees should obtain the legal instrument referred to, and have it registered without delay.

(2.) Every public school house and site are exempt from taxation, as provided in the Assessment Act. (R. S. O., sec. 6, cl. (5.)

7.—Registration of Trustees' Title to School Premises.

The trustees should not fail to register the title to their school site. In case the owner of a site refuses to sell and give them a title to it, and the trustees are compelled to take possession of it under an award of arbitrators, they should, on the affidavit of one of their number, verifying the same, register the award in the Registry Office. This should be done whenever they cannot obtain a conveyance of the property. (School Act, secs. 71 and 80.)

8.—When Trustees may sell a School Site or other Property.

School trustee corporations can dispose, by sale or otherwise, of any school site or school property which may not be required by them, in consequence of a change of school site; they should convey the same under their corporate seal. The proceeds of the sale are to be applied to lawful school purposes. All sites and other property, given or acquired for public school purposes, vest, therefore, absolutely in the trustee corporation for this purpose. (See "*School Sites*," chap. vii.)

9.—What constitutes adequate School Accommodation.

The law makes it the duty of trustees to provide adequate accommodation for "two-thirds of the actual resident children between the ages of 5 and 21 years, as ascertained by the census taken by the Municipal Council for the next preceding year." And now that the "compulsory" law is in force, this duty must be faithfully performed. (See sec. 2 of chap. viii.)

NOTE.—In case trustees fail to provide suitable outhouses, fences, maps, and tablets, inspectors should require that these deficiencies be supplied within a reasonable time; and unless reasonable and satisfactory efforts be made, having regard to the circumstances of each school, the defaulting trustees should be reported to the Department, in order to the consideration of the propriety of withholding the apportionment of the school fund from such section. (Minister Crooks' Decision, 1879.)

---

* Form of Deed for the site of the School House, Teacher's Residence, &c., can be obtained free of postage from Messrs. Copp, Clark & Co., Toronto, for 20 cents.

The accommodation, to be adequate, should include:

1. *Area of Site.*—A site of the area mentioned in note to section 1, chapter vii.

2. *Size of Rooms.*—The school house must be of the dimensions fixed by regulation. The area in each room shall be at least one hundred and twenty cubic feet of air for each child.* The rooms must also be sufficiently warmed and ventilated, and the premises properly drained.

3. *Separate Entrances.*—In school houses for more than fifty pupils, there should be separate entrances for boys and girls, with necessary cap and cloak rooms attached.

4. *Fence.*—A sufficient fence or paling round the school premises.

NOTE.—The *Ontario Line Fences Act* (R. S. O., ch. 198), which applies to school fences, enacts that "Owners of occupied adjoining lands shall make, keep up and repair a just proportion of the fence which marks the boundary between them; or, if there is no fence, they shall so make, keep up and repair the same proportion which is to mark such boundary; and owners of unoccupied, which adjoin occupied, lands, shall, upon their being occupied, be liable to the duty of keeping up and repairing such proportion, and in that respect shall be in the same position as if their land had been occupied at the time of the original fencing, and shall be liable to the compulsory proceedings hereinafter mentioned." (Sec. 2.) The Act further provides (in case of dispute) for the appointment of fence-viewers to make an award, which may be enforced as pointed out in the Statute.

5. *A Well*, or other means of procuring water for the school.

6. *Separate Offices.*—Proper and separate offices for both sexes, at some little distance from the school house and from each other, and enclosed, or otherwise masked.

7. *Furniture, Maps and Apparatus.*—Suitable school furniture and apparatus, desks, seats, blackboards, maps, presses, and books, &c., necessary for the efficient conduct of the school.

NOTE.—*General Suggestions to Trustees in regard to School House Lot.*—The school ground should, in the rural sections, embrace an acre in extent, and not less than half an acre, so as to allow the school house to be set well back from the road, and to furnish play-grounds within the fences. A convenient form for school grounds will be found to be an area of ten rods front by sixteen rods deep, with the school house set back four or six rods from the road. The grounds should be strongly fenced; the yards and outhouses in the rear of the school house should be separated by a high and tight board fence; the front grounds should also be planted with shade trees; shrubs and flowers in their season. Various simple plants, required for illustration in the lessons on botany, might be cultivated near the school house. Flowers, beautiful in themselves, have a most delightful and humanizing influence on children and youth, who should be taught to care for and preserve them from harm on the school premises.

---

* Thus, for instance, a room for fifty children would require space for 6,000 cubic feet of air. This would be equal to a cube of the following dimensions in feet, viz.: $30 \times 20 \times 10$, which is equivalent to a room 30 feet long by 20 feet wide and 10 feet high.

10.—Erection of School House, Teacher's Residence, &c.

The trustees alone have the right to decide upon the kind, size and description of the school house, or teacher's residence, which they shall erect. No ratepayer, public meeting, or committee has any authority to interfere with or control them in this matter. They have also full power to decide what fences, outbuildings, sheds and other accommodations shall be provided, as explained in section 9 of this chapter. To them also exclusively belongs the right to have the school grounds planted with shade trees and properly laid out.

11.—Restriction on the Use of the School House.

No school house or lot (unless so provided for in an old deed), or any building, furniture, or other thing pertaining thereto, shall be used or occupied for any other purpose than for the use and accommodation of the public school of the section or division, without the express permission of the trustee corporation, and then only after school hours, and on condition that all damages be made good, and cleaning, sweeping, &c., promptly done, or compensation made therefor.

NOTE.—Should trustees abuse this discretion in regard to the use of the school house, they may be restrained by injunction from the Courts.

12.—Duty in Regard to the Care and Repair of School House.

Trustees should, for convenience, appoint one of their number (or the Secretary-Treasurer or other responsible person), and give him authority, as well as make it his duty, to keep the school house in good repair. He should also see that the windows are properly filled with glass; that at a proper season the stove and pipe are in a fit condition, and suitable wood provided; that the desks and seats are in good repair; that the outhouses are properly provided with doors, and are frequently cleaned; that the blackboards are painted, the water supply abundant, and everything provided necessary for the comfort of the pupils and the efficiency of the school.

13.—Legal Decisions in Regard to the School.

(1.) *Trustees can levy a rate for the erection of a School House.*—The Court of Queen's Bench has decided that, under the School Act, school trustees are authorized to levy a rate for the erection of a school house in their section.—*Chief Superintendent of Education, appellant, in re Kelly v. Hedges, Burford, and 13 Windham.* 12 Q. B. R. 531.

(2.) *School House Contracts not valid without trustee Corporate Seal.*—The Court of Common Pleas has decided that the trustees of a School Section, being a corporation under the School Acts, are not liable as such to pay for a school house erected for and accepted by them, not having contracted under seal for the erection of the same. The seal is required as authenticating the concurrence of the whole body corporate.—*Marshall* v. *Trustees, No. 11 Kitley.* 4 C. P. R. 373.

NOTE.—Such a contract, not being binding on the corporation, would be binding on the individual trustees who made it with a third party, acting in good faith. *Query*, whether the trustee-corporation would not, by subsequently taking possession of the school house, or by some other act, recognize the validity of the contract?

(3). *Contract under Seal, signed by a majority of the Corporation, binding.*—The same Court has also decided the following case :—A contract was entered into by *two* of the trustees of a section under their corporate seal for building a school house ; after the house was built the trustees refused to pay, on the plea that the contract was not legal. A jury having given a verdict in favour of the trustees, a new trial was ordered, and the former verdict in favour of the trustees was set aside. The Court *held*, that a contract entered into by *two* trustees under the School Act, with the corporate seal attached, is sufficient ; and a plea that the contract was signed by the *two* subscribing trustees, with the consent or approbation of the *third*, was *held* bad.—*Forbes* v. *Trustees, No. 8, Plympton*. 8 C. P. R. 73, 74.

(4). *Alteration of Boundaries no valid ground for refusing to levy rates to pay for a School House.*—The same Court has decided the following case :—The plaintiff recovered a judgment in March, 1858, against the school trustees for a debt due to him for building a school house for the section, and made several unsuccessful attempts to obtain payment of the same from the trustees and their successors in office. The trustees always refused to levy a rate or to pay the judgment. To an application for a *mandamus* to compel the trustees to levy a rate for payment of the judgment, the Court *held* that it was no answer that, since the recovery of the judgment, two alterations had been made in the limits of the section, and that many changes had taken place among the rate-payers originally liable ; or that the merits of the claim on which the judgment was founded were capable of being impeached.—*Johnston* v. *School Trustees of Harwich*, 20 Q. B. 264, distinguished. *Scott* v. *Trustees, No. 1 Burgess, and 2 Bathurst*. 21 C. P. R. 398.

(5). *School House and Site in use not liable to be sold on judgment against Trustee Corporation.*—The Court of Queen's Bench has given judgment as follows :—In a case in which a school site had been given to the trustees for the purposes of a school (with the condition that it should revert to the giver in case it should cease to be used for school purposes), and on which they had erected a school house, judgment was obtained against the corporation for the money due on the building contract. The school house and site were actually sold and deeded by the Sheriff ; but the Court *held*, that the house and land could not lawfully be sold—it being contrary to public policy that a school house in daily use (any more than a court house or gaol) should be held liable upon a writ of execution, as, not the trustees, but the inhabitants of the section, are the *cestuis que trust* (*i. e.*, the persons for whose benefit the trust was held). The plaintiff should have resorted to his other remedies against the trustees for neglect of duty, &c. [as provided in the 252nd and 253rd sections of the Consolidated School Act of 1885.]—*Scott* v. *Trustees of Union Section No. 1 Burgess and 2 Bathurst*. 19 Q. B. R. 28.

(6). *Trespass on the School House.*—The Court of Queen's Bench has decided that the trustees of the school, and not the teacher, should sue for a trespass on the school house ; unless it can be shown that the trustees have given the teacher a particular interest in the building, beyond the mere liberty of occupying it during the day for the purpose of teaching.—*Monaghan* v. *Ferguson et al., London*. 3 Q. B. R. 484.

(7). *Use of School House.*—A bill was filed by a rate-payer, seeking to restrain school trustees from allowing the school house to be used for religious services ; but the bill did not allege that it was filed on behalf of the plaintiff and all other rate-payers. Two of the three school trustees consented to the injunction being granted as asked. The Court refused the application on the grounds—first, that the suit was not properly constituted ; and that if it had been, it appearing that a majority of the trustees were in favour of the views of the plaintiff, they had themselves the power to do that which they consented to the Court doing. *Quære*, if the bill had been by the plaintiff on behalf of himself and all other rate-payers, whether then the suit would have been properly constituted ?—*Rabian* v. *The School Trustees, Thurlow*. 12 Chy. 115.

(8.) *Proposed School House—Submission to Electors—Sufficiency of Submission.*
— t appeared from affidavit of the Secretary and Treasurer of a school section, that at two regularly called meetings of the only qualified electors of a school section at which a chairman was appointed, proposals to purchase a site, build a school house, and borrow money therefor, were put by way of motion and carried, upon which a by-law was passed authorizing the issue of debentures to raise money for the above purposes.

Held, by Armour, J., that under 42 Vict., cap. 34, sec. 29, subs. 3, this was a sufficient submission to, and approval of the the proposal by the duly qualified electors of the section, and a rule to quash the by-law was discharged.—*In re McCormick and the Corporation of the Township of Colchester South.* C. L. S., I., 215.

(9.) *Public School—Transfer of Pupil—Want of Accommodation—Mandamus.*
—A child was registered at one of the public schools in the town of Windsor, and attended thereat during the last school term; on 3rd September last the plaintiff, her father, made application for her admission into the other school, which being refused, he applied for a mandamus. By the Public School Regulations, cap. 12, sec. 6, it is declared that a registered pupil shall continue at the school at which he has been registered till regularly withdrawn; by sec. 7 the inspector may transfer pupils. The plaintiff had not complied with these regulations.

Held, by Ferguson, J., that he was not entitled to a mandamus.

It appeared that the school to which he sought admission for his child did not afford accommodation for her.

Held, a sufficient ground for refusing the mandamus.—*Dunn v. The School Board of Windsor,* C. L. J., iii., 551.

(10). *The Assessment Act* exempts from taxation "every public school house, with the land attached thereto, and the personal property belonging to it." (Sec. 9, cl. 5.)

NOTE.—See chapter vi. on "School Meetings," and section 15 of chapter vii., containing Decision of the Courts in regard to School sites.

III.—POWER AND DUTIES OF TRUSTEES IN REGARD TO THE SCHOOL TEACHERS, &c.

14.—Providing Teacher, Apparatus, Books, School Bell, &c.

The trustees alone, and not any public meeting, have the right to decide what teacher shall be employed, how much shall be paid to him; what apparatus, library, prize and text books shall be purchased; what repairs; that contingent expenses for stationery, postage, warming and cleaning the school houses, purchase of school bell, &c., shall be authorized, (as explained in the next section of this chapter;) in short, they alone have the right to decide upon everything which they may think expedient to do in order to promote the interests of the school.

15.—Who shall determine the Expenses of the School.

The majority of the trustees of every school section have, as we have shown, the sole right to decide as to what expenses they will incur for maps, school furniture, apparatus, library and prize books;

salaries of teachers, rent of school house, cost of school bell; warming, cleaning, repairs, contingent and all other expenses of their school. The trustees, as explained in the preceding section, are not required to refer such matters to any public meeting whatever; and no resolutions of a public meeting on the subject have any legal force, especially as the schools are now free by law. (See sec. 1 of chap. xiii.)

16.—Trustees to establish Free Public School Library.

Trustees should, under the general regulations, establish a free public school library for the children and ratepayers of their section. They can appoint and pay any competent person to act as librarian. In case they do not appoint any such person, the teacher is required, without additional salary, to act as librarian *ex-officio* for the section. (See chapter ix., relating to teachers.)

NOTE.—The property of every public library is exempt from taxation.

17.—Fees Chargeable on all Non-Residents.

The children of all non-residents alike, whether ratepayers of the section or not, must now pay a school fee per calendar month in advance, not exceeding fifty cents per pupil. (See section 207 of the School Act of 1885.) This applies to non-resident children who reside nearer to the school concerned than to "the school in their own section.* In case of dispute as to distance from the school, the inspector shall decide.

18.—Authorized Text Books only can be used.

The School Act makes it the duty of trustees "To see that no unauthorized text books are used in the school, and that the pupils are duly supplied with a uniform series of authorized text books, sanctioned by the Education Department. (Sec. 40, cl. 11.) The Act further declares that no teacher shall use or permit to be used as text books in a model or public school any books except such as are authorized by the Education Department. (*Ibid.* sec. 210; see also sec. 4 of chap. xiii.)

NOTE.—Teachers or other persons who shall negligently or wilfully substitute any unauthorized text book * * * shall be liable to a penalty not exceeding ten dollars. (*Ibid.* sec. 212.) A change, however, may be made at the beginning of a term by consent of the trustees and inspector. (*Ibid.* sec. 211.)

19.—Trustees' Visitation to the School.—Registers, &c.

The Act requires the trustees "to visit, from time to time, every school under their charge, and see that it is conducted according to

---

* The School Act of 1885 makes a special exception as to non-resident pupils attending a public school in any city, town or incorporated village. Such pupils shall for all matters affecting the division of the legislative or municipal grants be reported as attending the public school of the school section in which they are actual residents. (School Act, sec. 207, cl. 2.) The trustees and teacher of a school at which non-resident ratepayers' children attend, must see that the law is complied with in this respect.

law and the authorized regulations, and to provide school registers and a visitors' book, in the forms prescribed by the Education Department." (Sec. 40, cl. 10.)

NOTE.—These registers can be obtained through the inspectors gratuitously.

NOTE.—The individual power of a trustee in a school is limited. It does not include any right on his part to interfere with the teacher in his administration of discipline in the school, or in his mode of teaching. The teacher is not subject to the direction of an individual trustee, unless acting under the express authority of both of his colleagues. Trustees should not reprove or censure a teacher in the presence of any of his pupils.

20.—Two or more Schools may be established.

Trustees are authorized " to select a site for and establish and maintain an additional school or additional schools in the section, with the concurrence of the inspector, where, from the large size of the section, its physical conformation, or from any other cause, the children of the section are unable to attend the school established therein." (Sec. 74, cl. 2.) Under the "compulsory" provisions of the Act this additional school may often be a necessity, as authorized by the School Act, section 40, cl. (5).

21.—Duty of Trustees and Teacher to report to the Inspector.

The law declares that a school section shall forfeit its share of the school fund, and the trustees become personally responsible for such loss, should they or the teacher fail to furnish the inspector with a full and satisfactory report every six months, and at the end of the year, in the form provided. (Sec. 263.)

22.—Orders to be given to qualified Teachers only.

Trustees employing qualified teachers, assistants, or monitors, should give them the necessary orders upon the county inspector for the school fund apportioned and payable to their school section, but they should not give an order in favour of any teacher (assistant or monitor), except for the actual time during which said teacher, (assistant or monitor,) while employed, held a legal certificate of qualification.

NOTE.—Trustees sometimes omit the giving of such orders, and thus, designedly or unwittingly, evade the law. They do so for one of three reasons, viz.: (1), if they have themselves advanced the money to the teacher; or (2), have paid him by orders on a store; or (3), if they have employed a teacher without the legal qualifications. None of these reasons are valid. The order on the county inspector should therefore be given. In case it is refused the trustees can be sued for refusal to give the order (and not for the money due), as decided by the Court of Queen's Bench.

CHAPTER III.

POWERS AND DUTIES OF A SCHOOL SECRETARY-TREASURER AND COLLECTOR.

1.—Appointment and Duties of a Secretary-Treasurer.

The secretary-treasurer appointed by the trustees shall give such security as may be required by a majority of the board. The trustees shall deposit the security for safe keeping with the clerk of the township council. (School Act, secs. 33 and 260.) The object of the appointment of a secretary-treasurer is:—

(1.) *Production of Papers.*—For the production ("when called for by the trustees, auditors or other competent authority,) of the papers and moneys belonging to the corporation." (*Ibid.* sec. 34.)

(2.) *Record of Proceedings.*—For "the keeping of a correct record of all the proceedings of every meeting of the trustees in a minute book procured by them for that purpose, and to see that the minutes, when confirmed, are signed by the presiding trustee." (*Ibid.*)

(3.) *Accounts for Moneys.*—For the receiving and accounting for "all school moneys collected from the inhabitants or ratepayers of the school section, or other persons." (*Ibid.*)

(4.) *Payment of Moneys.*—For the disbursing of such "moneys in the manner directed by the majority of the trustees." (*Ibid.*)

(5.) For calling the ordinary meetings of the trustee board, and "at the request in writing of two trustees, a special meeting of the board of trustees." (*Ibid.*)

NOTE.—Notice of all meetings shall be given by the secretary to each of the trustees, or by any one of the trustees to the others, by notifying them personally, or in writing, or by sending a written notice to their residences. (*Ibid.* sec. 35.)

Notifying the trustees personally is always a doubtful method, as, without witness to the fact, it is often incapable of proof in case of denial.

(6.) For receiving a statement of the school census of the section from the township clerk. (*Ibid.* sec. 118.)

(7.) *Repair of House.*—And for seeing to the repair of the school house, and care of the school premises if desired by the trustees. (See sec. 12 of chap. ii.)

2.—Secretary-Treasurer or Trustee to Account—Penalty.

Should any secretary-treasurer or trustee wrongfully withhold, neglect or refuse at any time to deliver up, or to account for and pay over, any books, papers, chattels or moneys which came into his possession as such secretary-treasurer, or trustee or otherwise, * * * * or any part thereof to the person, and in the manner directed by a majority of the school trustees for the school section then in office, or by other competent authority, such withholding, neglect or refusal shall be punishable. (Sec. 262.) And the county judge is authorized, on the application and affidavit of two trustees or two ratepayers, to "order the person complained of to deliver up, account for and pay over the books, papers, chattels or moneys, by a certain day to be named by the judge, upon pain of imprisonment, without bail, until the order is complied with. (*Ibid*, secs. 263-265.)

3.—Decisions of the Courts in Regard to the Secretary-Treasurer.

(1.) *Defaulting Secretary-Treasurer.*—The Court of Queen's Bench has also decided that a trustee corparation could maintain an action "for money had and received," against their secretary-treasurer, to recover money in his hands not expended or accounted for.—*Trustees of Section 7, Stephen* v. *Mitchell*, 29 Q. B. R., 382.

(2.) *Liability of a Secretary-Treasurer and his Surety.*—One T., who acted in the capacity of secretary-treasurer of the plaintiffs, who had not been appointed in writing, and had not given security as required by the statute in that behalf, absconded with certain moneys which had been received by him as such secretary-treasurer, from the defendants. The plaintiffs had recognized T. as their secretary-treasurer by entrusting him with the custody of their books and papers, by allowing him to receive moneys for them, by auditing his accounts and receiving and approving of the auditor's reports. *Held*, that R. S. O., c. 204, s. 29, which provides that, in the case of a rural school section corporation, the resolution, action or proceeding of at least two of the trustees shall be necessary in order lawfully to bind such corporation, does not apply to acts of duty of the secretary-treasurer; and that payment by the municipality of school moneys to T. was binding on the trustees. *Held*, also, that if a person acts notoriously as the officer of a corporation, and is recognized by it as such officer, a regular appointment will be presumed, and his acts will bind the corporation, although no written proof is, or can be, adduced of his appointment.—*School Trustees of the Township of Hamilton* v. *Neil*, 28 Chy., 204.

A municipal corporation passed a by-law for raising a loan to liquidate a debt to be incurred in enlarging the school-house in a public school section, and providing for the issue of debentures for that purpose, and for levying a special rate to pay the interest thereon, and to create a sinking fund for the payment of the principal; and the municipal authorities paid the money so raised by the said special rate to the secretary-treasurer of the school board of the said section. A, the secretary-treasurer of the school board, and B, as his surety, gave a bond of office, reciting that A had been appointed such secretary-treasurer, and that "it was required that security should be given for the due and faithful performance of any and all the duties pertaining to such office," and conditioned to "correctly and safely keep any and all moneys and papers belonging to the said school board, and to faithfully and honestly deliver up, account for, and pay over any moneys which at any time thereafter might come into his hands and possession as such secretary-treasurer. *Held*, that the condition must be read with reference to the recital, and its scope might be thereby restricted, and reading the two together B was not liable for the moneys so received by A, which were outside the duties pertaining to his office, and should have been retained by the municipal corporation. B having been informed by the school board that A was in default, but not in respect of what moneys the default was made, as to which he made no enquiries, and having at the request of the school board given a mortgage to secure the liability which he was informed he had, by reason of such default, incurred as surety under the above bond, and having subsequently ascertained that the default was partly in respect of moneys so improperly paid to A. *Held*, that B was entitled to redeem on payment of the balance only of the moneys for which he was held liable as surety, the mortgage having been executed under a mistake.—*Keith* v. *Fenelon Falls Union School Section et al.*, 3 O. R., Chy. D., 194.

(3.) *Personal Liability of Secretary-Treasurer in regard to withholding Books, &c.*—*Held*, that an award made by arbitrators appointed under sec. 29 of C. S. U. C., c. 64, against one of the trustees (the secretary-treasurer), in his individual capacity as said trustee, for wrongfully withholding books, moneys, &c., is binding; 2. That the citing of a trustee to appear before the judge of the County Court, under sec. 130 *et seq*, of the School Act, is not necessarily a bar to proceeding by arbitration under sec. 29; and 3. That under sec. 130, the judge of the County Court has no jurisdiction, except when a secretary-treasurer "has in his possession books, moneys, &c., which came into his possession as secretary-treasurer, and which he wrongfully holds and refuses to deliver up, &c.," and such secretary-treasurer must be guilty of misdemeanour, contemplated by the 130th clause, before the judge can interfere.—*Ferris* v. *Chesterfield et al.*, 10 C. P. 272; 6 L. J. 163.

4.—School Collector of Non-Residents' Fees.

Section 207 requires the fees of non-resident pupils to be paid in advance, but as this is not always done, it may be desirable for the trustees to appoint a person to act as collector of them. The trustees should pay a reasonable fee for this service.

5.—Trustee School Warrant to Collectors.

Should the fees, or rate bill, of non-residents not be paid in advance or when demanded, the trustees should make out a list of defaulters, and give to the collector a warrant for the collection of the several sums mentioned in such list.*

Where school fees are charged in a rate bill to non-residents, as authorized by law, the following directions should be followed:—

(1.) *Remarks on the Rate Bill.*—As no rate bill on non-residents can exceed 50 cents per calendar month for each pupil, payable in advance, the whole charge for school fees, including collector's charge, cannot exceed this amount. The collector's fees must be paid by the trustees out of the amount collected, or from the general funds of the section.

NOTE.— The form for this Rate Bill can be obtained, free of postage, from Messrs. Copp, Clark & Co., Front Street, Toronto, for 5 cents.

(2.) Teachers can have no legal claim to these fees as an extra allowance or perquisite, unless the trustees agree beforehand to pay them over to the teachers. They should go into the general funds of the section.

(3.) The collector should take a receipt from the secretary-treasurer of the section for all fees paid to him. The secretary-treasurer should also take a receipt from the teacher for all moneys paid to him.

NOTE.—The taking and giving of receipts for moneys paid and received will prevent errors and misunderstandings.

---

* Forms of the Bond and Security given by a secretary-treasurer can be supplied by Messrs. Copp, Clark & Co., Front Street, Toronto, free by post, at the following rate:—

Bond of Secretary-Treasurer .. .. 5 cents.

(4.) When the payment of the rate bill is made to the teacher, it should be authorized by the trustees. The teacher should, of course, apprize the collector of all payments made to him, so that he (the collector) may not be at the trouble of calling upon such persons.

6.—Rate Bills on Non-Residents.

No rate bill for fuel, or any other contingency, can be collected from parents or guardians. But a rate bill for tuition must be charged for all non resident children who attend. (Secs. 207 and 128; see also sec. 17 of chapter ii., and sec. 5 of this chapter.)

NOTE.—Rate bills (not exceeding twenty cents per month, per pupil) for text books, stationery, fuel and other contingencies, may be collected from parents or guardians in cities, towns and villages. (See School Act, sec. 117, cl. 7.)

7.—Duties and Liabilities of Collectors of School Fees.

Collector shall call for the Fees.—The collector, on receiving his list, should call on the non-residents, or send by post a statement of the demand. The entry of the date of such demand on his roll opposite the name, shall be *prima facie* proof of the demand.

8.—Defraying expenses of the School.

School Trustees have now no power to collect rates on property to defray the expenses of their schools. They must apply to the Township Council for any sums which they may require. The provisions of the School law of 1885 on this subject are as follows:—

"To apply to the Township Council at or before its meeting in August for the levying and collecting by rate, all sums for the support of their school, or schools, and for any other school purposes authorized by this Act to be collected from the ratepayers of such section." (Sch. Act, sec. 40, cl. 3.)

NOTE.—Section 121 requires the Township Council to levy and collect on the taxable property in each section such * * * sums as may be required by the Trustees thereof for school purposes."*—(*Ibid.* sec. 121.)

In this way the ordinary annual current expenses of the school are provided for; but in case special expenditures are contemplated the law provides that the Trustees shall apply to the Township Council—"to raise the amount necessary for the purchase of school sites, the erection or otherwise acquiring of school-houses and their appendages and teacher's residence, either by one yearly rate or by debentures, as provided in section one hundred and thirty-three, and one hundred

---

* See NOTE to section 9 of this chapter.
A proper form of "estimate" and requisition to be laid before the Township Council by Trustees, can be obtained from Messrs. Copp, Clark & Co., Toronto, or any bookseller, for 5 cents.
Where Township Councils authorize a school loan to be made by School Trustees, they are required to issue debentures for the amount of such loan. Forms of such debentures, with coupons attached, can be obtained from Messrs. Copp, Clark & Co., Toronto, or other booksellers, for 15 cents.

and thirty-five of this Act, as may be required by the Trustees. (*Ibid.*)

NOTE.—The consent of the ratepayers to the levying of the rate by the Township Council for "current expenses" (as distinguished from expenses for building, etc.) is not necessary, as already explained.

In all cases the Township Council should add the amount of the collector's fees and other expenses of collection to the rate to be levied, so as to enable the Council to hand over the exact sum asked for by the Trustees. This sum the trustees can lawfully claim, and can sue for it in case the full amount is not paid over to them by the Council irrespective of fees.

9.—Special Expenditures for School House, etc.

The 133rd section of the Act is as follows:—"On the application of any Board of Rural School Trustees for the issue of debentures for the purchase of a school site or sites, for the erection of a school-house or school-houses, or for the purchase or erection of a teacher's residence, the Municipal Council of the Township shall pass a By-law for the said purpose, and shall forthwith issue a debenture or debentures to be repayable out of the taxable property of the school section concerned, and subject to the limitations contained in this Act. (*Ibid,* sec. 133.)

The limitations are contained in the following section:—

"The Municipal Council of any township shall not borrow or levy, or collect any rate for any sum of money for any of the purposes mentioned in this [next preceding] section unless the proposal for the same has been submitted by the Trustees to and approved of at a special meeting of the duly qualified school electors of this section called for that purpose." (*Ibid.* sec. 134.)

The school meeting has the right to object to a loan by the Trustees, or to the levy of a rate by the Township Council, for the purposes mentioned above. In other words, it has full power to discuss with the Trustees, and decide with them upon the expediency of the proposed outlay, its amount, or any particular item in the estimate. The final result of the discussion at the meeting should be embodied in formal resolutions for the guidance of the Trustees, and on which they can, if the outlay be approved, base their estimate and requisition to the Township Council.

When the proposed loan or rate for expenditure has been sanctioned by the school meeting, the Trustees can compel the Township Council (in case of its refusal) by *mandamus*, from the High Court of Justice, to raise the amounts required, as agreed to at the special meeting.

Discretion is given by the following section to the Township Council in regard to the time at which the debentures necessary for these purposes shall be issued:—

"No Township Council shall levy or collect in any school section during any one year more than one school section rate except for the purpose of a school site, or for the erection of a school-house." (Sch. Act, sec. 137.)

10.—Township Special Assessment for each School.

In order to stimulate Trustees to keep up a good school, provision is made in section 121 of the School Act for a permissive special assessment in aid of each school as follows :—

"The Municipal Council of every township may levy and collect by assessment, upon the taxable property of the public school supporters of the township, in the manner provided by this Act, and by the Municipal and Assessment Acts and amendments, the sum of one hundred dollars for every public school section therein in which a school has been kept open the whole year exclusive of vacations (a proportionate sum being levied for a shorter term, and an additional sum of fifty dollars for each additional teacher employed the whole year)" (*Ibid.* sec. 21.)

11.—For what a Section School Rate may be Collected.

Township councils can collect rates for any of the school purposes enumerated in sections 9 to 12, inclusive, of chapter ii.

12.—For what a Section School Rate cannot be Collected.

No rate can be lawfully levied :—

1. *Teacher's Salary.*—To pay the salary of any master or assistant teacher, who does not, during the whole time for which the salary is claimed by such teacher, etc., possess a legal certificate of qualification. (School Act, sec. 157.)

2. *Trustee's Claim.*—To pay any claim of a co-trustee for anything except a school site, or as remuneration for acting as a collector of school rates. (*Ibid.* sec. 253.)

3. *Cost of Suits.*—To pay costs of an illegal suit, or for unsuccessfully defending a suit brought against them for illegal acts, as decided by the Court of Queen's Bench, 14 Q. B. R. 473.

4. *Unnecessary Expenses.*—For unnecessary travelling expenses, &c.

5. *For excessive Interest, i.e.* over eight per cent., and the expenses of unauthorized loans, &c.

NOTE.—In the case of *Malcolm* v. *Malcolm* (15 Chy. 13), the Court of Chancery declared it was "contrary to the rule of this court, in dealing with persons who have not acted properly, to punish them more severely than justice to others renders necessary ; and therefore where school trustees wrongfully expended money in building on a site which had been changed by competent authority, relief was only granted to a ratepayer who complained of the act, subject to equitable terms and conditions."

13.—Application to Township Council to Collect Rates.

Before authorizing any school rate, the trustees should decide before hand whether the money required by them is (1) for current expenses, or (2) on capital account, as authorized by the ratepayers. In either case an estimate of the sum required by the trustees in the former case should be sent to the township council, at or before its August meeting. (Sec. 40.) The council, upon receiving the trustees' estimate for current expenses, and a request in writing, must levy the required rate within a reasonable time, and pay it over to the trustees (without any diminution of the collector's fees or expenses—which must be added to the rate itself by the council).

NOTE.—In case of refusal, on the part of a township council, to levy the amount required by the trustees, the remedy is by mandamus from either the Court of Queen's Bench or Common Pleas. (Decisions of the Courts on this subject are given in Part II. of these Lectures, and also an analysis of the whole school law in regard to township councils.)

☞ Blank forms of estimates and requisitions on the township council can be sent by post by Messrs. Copp, Clark & Co., Front Street, Toronto, for 10 cents per sheet.

For the special expenditure the council must issue a debenture, or debentures, for the sum to be borrowed, and provide the means for securing repayment of the amount borrowed, by a yearly rate imposed in the manner specified in the Act.

14.—Decisions of the Courts in Regard to School Rates.

(1.) *Township Treasurer—Bond—Moneys for general uses of Municipality—Deficit in School Moneys—Liability of Sureties.*—The bond of a Township Treasurer, dated 6th of October, 1874, was conditioned to pay over for the use of the Municipality all moneys coming to his hands by virtue of his office, and applicable to the general uses of the Municipality. A deficit occured in Clergy Reserve moneys and moneys derived from the distribution of the Provincial Surplus. By two by-laws of the Municipality, passed in 1859 and 1875, these two funds were set apart for educational purposes, and directed to be invested and the interest distributed "amongst the several school divisions as the Township Council shall direct."

Held, on the chancellor that as there is a plainly recognized distinction between municipal moneys specifically appropriated and those unappropriated, *prima facie* these funds being appropriated to educational purposes ceases to be applicable to general uses or purposes of the corporation, and as against the sureties to the bond were not within its condition.

Held, also, that the operation of the bond was not enlarged by R. S. O. cap. 180, sec 213, and cap. 204, sec 221, which refers only to Treasurers of Counties, Cities, and Towns, and not to Township Treasurers.—*Townships of Oakland v. Prosser.* I. O. R. div. D. 330.

(2.) *Requisition to Municipal Councils for Funds for School Site.*—A municipal corporation has no discretion in accepting or rejecting the requisition of school trustees for funds for a school site, except by a two-thirds vote. An adverse vote by a smaller majority is a virtual acceptance, and the requisition must therefore be complied with.—*Re Board of Education of Napanee and the Corporation of the town of Napanee*, 29 Chy., £95.

To a bill by a rural school section corporation to compel the municipality to make good money paid by the municipality to a person alleged not to be the duly appointed officer of the corporation, the treasurer of the municipality is not a proper party.—*School Trustees of the Township of Hamilton v. Neil*, 28 Chy., 408.

(3.) *Mandamus to levy School Rates to School Trustees.*—The court refused a mandamus to compel school trustees to pay a sum awarded to be due to a teacher for arrears of salary, observing that there were other remedies open. Upon the facts also, which are stated in the case, the legality of the award appears doubtful.—*O'Leary and the Trustees of School Section No. 2, in the Township of Blandford,* 19 Q. B. 556.

(4.) *Mandamus to levy School Rates to Municipal Corporations.*—K. was employed in 1848 by the trustees of school section 4, in the township of Sandwich, acting under a by-law of the district council, to furnish materials for and to erect a school house in that section. Part of the money was paid to him on account, and for the balance he recovered judgment against the trustees. Finding no property on which to levy, he applied in 1859 to the municipal council, who passed a by-law imposing a rate to satisfy his judgment; but this by-law was repealed before the money had been collected. It appears that, under the original by-law of the district council, the rate for erecting the school house had been levied, and the part not paid over to K. had been handed to the secretary-treasurer of the trustees, who absconded, and that K. was in possession of the school house, and retained it for the money due him:—*Held,* that the township council were not liable; and a mandamus to them to pass a by-law for raising money to satisfy the claim, was refused *Semble,* also, that if the applicant were entitled to recover, an action would lie against the council, and therefore no mandamus should go.—*Kennedy* v. *Municipal Council of the Township of Sandwich,* 9 Q. B. 326.

CHAPTER IV.

THE LAW RELATING TO NON-RESIDENTS.

1.—A Resident of a School Section Defined.

(1.) A person who has his home, domicile, or place of business in a section or other school division, and on which he pays taxes, is a resident; (2) A non-resident who pays "the average school rate" to the section of an actual resident (School Act, sec. 2, cl. (6); (3) Apprentices; and (4) *bonâ fide* settlers whose names are not yet on the assessment roll, are to be regarded as residents.

2.—A Non-Resident of a School Section Defined.

A "non-resident" of a school section or division, is, strictly speaking, one who does not reside in it. But a person (as in No. 2 above) may be a legal "resident" of a section, and have a right to vote at its school meetings and not yet reside in it. Transient visitors, children who leave home and come to remain in a section or division for a short time, and inmates of school age in a house of refuge (School Act, sec 208) are non-residents.

NOTE.— Any resident claiming to be the guardian of a non-resident or other child that may come to live with him, must satisfy the trustees, by documentary or other legal proof, of the validity of his claim to be such guardian.

3.—Non-Residents Liable for Rates in their own Section.

A person paying rates in the section in which he resides does not thereby relieve himself from the payment of rates in any other school section in which he owns property and is taxed. (School Act, sec. 128.)

4.—Rights of the Non-Resident Ratepayers of a Section.

A non-resident ratepayer of a section (defined above (2) as a resident) has a right to send his children or wards (if he be a guardian), to the school of any section in which he pays school rates without any additional charge. (*Ibid*, sec. 2, cl. (6.) See section 17, chapter ii.)

NOTE.—The children of a non-resident "attending a public school in any city, town or incorporated village, shall be reported as attending the public school of the school section in which they are actual residents."—(*Ibid*, sec. 207, cl. (2.)

5.—Authority of Trustees in regard to Non-Residents.

Trustees are required to admit the children of non-residents to their school on payment in advance of a rate bill of fifty cents per child per calendar month, (See sec. 17, ch. ii.) Should the non-residents reside nearer to the school than to the one in their own section, the trustees must admit them on the payment of the fee. In case of any dispute as to the comparative distance from the school, the inspector has power to finally decide the matter. (*Ibid*, sec. 207.)

NOTE.—Supporters of Roman Catholic separate schools, have no right to send their children to the public school while they are supporters of these schools.

6.—Rates on Non-Residents owning Property.

(1.) *Non-Residents.*—Non-residents owning taxable property in the section are as liable as other ratepayers. (*Ibid*, secs, 2, cl. (6), and 128.)

CHAPTER V.

SCHOOL SECTION AUDITORS—ACCOUNTABILITY OF TRUSTEES AND OTHERS.

1.—When and by whom School Auditors are appointed.

The law requires the Trustees of each section, "on or before the first day of December, to appoint an auditor, and in case of their neglect, or the neglect of the ratepayers to do so, or in case of an auditor being appointed, or elected, who refuses to act, then the inspector, at the request in writing of any two ratepayers, shall make such appointment." (Sch. Act, sec. 37.)

2.—Auditor's time of Meeting, and object of it.

The auditors chosen, "or one of them, shall, on, or immediately after, the first day of December, in each year, appoint a time before the day of the next ensuing annual school meeting, for examining the accounts of the school section." (*Ibid.* sec. 38.) They should, of course, apprise the Secretary-Treasurer of the Trustees of the day fixed for examining the accounts.

3.—The object of the School Audit, and duty of the Auditors.

Is "to examine into and decide upon the accuracy of the accounts of such section, and whether the Trustees have truly accounted for, and expended for school purposes, the moneys received by them." (Sch. Act, sec. 39, cl 1.)

4.—Duration of the Time of the Audit.

In case of delay in completing the audit, even beyond the year of appointment, the law declares that "the auditors shall remain in office *until their audit is completed.*" (*Ibid.* sec. 39, cl. 4, (*d*).)

5.—When, and to whom, are the Auditors to Report.

The auditors are required to submit the school accounts of the section, with a full report thereon, to the next annual school meeting. (*Ibid.* sec. 39, cl. 1.)

NOTE.—In case collusion should be found to exist between the auditors of a rural school section and the trustees in regard to their accounts, or in case of any other alleged irregularity in the school accounts, any two ratepayers can, under the authority of the 263rd and following sections of the Public Schools Act, 1885, apply to the judge of the County Court to summon witnesses and hold an inquiry into the facts, and take evidence in regard thereto under oath. (Minister Crooks' Decision, 1879.)

6.—What the School Auditors have authority to do.

Any School Auditor can "require the attendance of all, or any of the persons interested in the accounts, and of their witnesses, with all such books, papers and writings as such auditor (or auditors) may direct them, or either of them, to produce." The auditors may "administer oaths to such persons and witnesses." They have also full power to enforce by warrant "the collection of any moneys by them awarded to be paid." (*Ibid.* sec. 39, cl. 4.)

7.—Obligation on Trustees and others to furnish Information.

The law declares that "the trustees, or their secretary-treasurer, in their behalf, shall not refuse to furnish the auditors of any accounts of a rural school section, or either of them, with any papers or information in their power, and which may be required of them, relative to their school accounts, and any contravention of this section upon prosecution therefor [before a magistrate] by either of the auditors or any ratepayer, shall be punished by fine or imprisonment." (*Ibid.* sec. 267.)

8.—Obligations on Trustees and other parties to Account.

The School Act also declares that no secretary-treasurer * * * and no person having been such secretary-treasurer, and no trustee, or other person who may have in his possession any books, papers, chattels or moneys which came into his possession as such secretary-treasurer, trustee, or otherwise shall wrongfully withhold or neglect, or refuse to deliver up or account for and pay over the same or any part thereof to the person and in the manner directed by a majority of the school trustees. Upon proof of such wrongful withholding or refusal, the County Judge shall order the party complained of to deliver up, account for and pay over, the books, papers, chattels or moneys applied for, by a certain day, with reasonable costs, on pain of imprisonment by the sheriff, without bail. (*Ibid.* secs. 262-265.)

9.—Responsibility of Trustees and others for Lost Moneys.

If it can be proved at the audit, or at any other time, that "any part of the public school fund or moneys be embezzled or lost, through the dishonesty or faithlessness of any trustee, secretary-treasurer, or other person to whom it has been entrusted, and proper security against the loss shall not have been taken, the person or persons whose duty it was to have exacted the security shall be *personally responsible* for the sum so embezzled or lost; and such sums may be recovered from him or them by the person entitled to receive the same, by action at law in any court having jurisdiction to the amount, or by information at the suit of the Crown." (*Ibid.* sec. 261; see *Ferris* v. *Irwin*, No. 16 Darlington, 10 C. P. R., 116, in regard to Embezzlement by Trustees.)

10.—Lawfulness or Expediency of Trustees' Expenditure.

The two auditors may object to the *lawfulness*, but not to the expediency of any expenditure. The trustees are the sole judges as to the *expediency* of such expenditure. It is only when both of the auditors object to the lawfulness of an expenditure (that is, whether the expenditure is authorized by the School Law, or comes fairly within the objects of the trust), that it is necessary to submit the matter for the decision of the school meeting, which may either determine the same, or submit it to the Minister for final decision. (*Ibid.* sec. 39, cl. 3.)

NOTE.—"In case of difference of opinion between the auditors on any matter in the account, it shall be referred to and decided by the county inspector." (*Ibid.* sec. 39, cl. 2.)

11.—What are Lawful School Section Expenditures?

The "expenditure" of a school may be "for any lawful purpose whatsoever," and may not only include the ordinary expenses of the school, but also collector's fees, law costs incurred in maintaining or defending necessary suits, postages, stationery, or any incidentals connected with the office of trustees.

NOTE.—While trustees carry out the lawful decision of their constituents, neither the auditors nor any public meeting can limit or deprive them of the authority conferred upon them by the Act, "as to keeping in repair and order the section school house, and its furniture and appendages." (*Ibid-* sec. 40, cl. (5); see also sections 6 and 7 of chapter iii.)

12.—Summary in regard to Audit of School Section Accounts.

The law requires trustees, or their secretary-treasurer, to lay all their accounts before the school auditors of the section, with all the vouchers, contracts, agreements, books, and verbal information, under oath, if necessary, on the subject of the receipts and expenditure, as may serve to explain the items in the accounts. (*Ibid.* sec. 37, cl. 2.)

13.—Summary of Duties and Powers of Rural School Trustees.*

The duties which trustees are required to perform, as well as their discretionary powers, may be summarized as follows :—

(1.) To call the annual school meeting ; also a special one to fill up a vacancy in the office of trustee.

(2.) To call special school meetings to decide the question of school site.

(3.) To call a special school meeting for any lawful school purpose.

(4.) To prosecute all illegal voters at school meetings.

(5.) To make a verbal declaration of office, after knowledge of election as trustee, and before entering on its duties.

---

* The provision of the law prescribing the duty of trustees in regard to compulsory education, will be found in chapter viii.

(6.) To see that their school is furnished with a trustees' book, a visitors' book, the entrance, daily class and general registers, and an educational periodical, at the expense of the school. (School Act, sec. 40, cl. 11.)

(7.) To appoint at their discretion an officer to make an annual return of all the children in their school section or division who do not attend any school. (*Ibid.* sec. 217.) *

(8.) To charge absentee pupils not more than one dollar per month for such absence, or report the case to a magistrate. (*Ibid.* sec. 221.)

(9.) To provide suitable school accommodation for all the pupils in their section, as defined in the regulations. (*Ibid.* sec. 40, cl. 2.)

(10.) To employ and pay school moneys to none but legally qualified teachers and assistants. (*Ibid.*)

(11.) To permit all pupils between the age of five and twenty-one years, on whose behalf school rates are paid, and who observe the rules, to attend their school. (*Ibid.*)

(12.) To fix a rate bill of fifty cents each, per calendar month (payable in advance), upon all of the children of non-residents who are sent to their school (*Ibid.* sec. 207.)

(13.) To visit the school and see that it is properly conducted; that no unauthorized books are used; that all the pupils are properly supplied with proper text books. (*Ibid.* sec. 40, cl. 10.)

(14.) To exercise all the corporate powers vested in them, for the fulfilment of all agreements, contracts, &c.; and to maintain a school in their section during the year.

(15.) To transmit their *half-yearly* returns and their *yearly* reports to the inspector, and also to submit their *yearly* report to the annual meeting of their constituents.

(16.) To affix their corporate seal to all contracts, agreements, deeds, &c., under their hand.

(17.) To appoint and take proper security from the secretary-treasurer and school collector.

(18.) To make a return to the municipal clerk of all rate bills imposed by them.

(19.) To make no contract with any member of the school corporation, except for school site, or as collector.

(20.) To transact no school business except at a trustee meeting, of which each member of the corporation has had due notice.

(21.) To appoint a school auditor before the 1st of December in each year, and lay before the auditors all necessary information.

---

* The provision of the law prescribing the duty of trustees in regard to compulsory education will be found in chapter viii.

Chap. V.]   ACCOUNTABILITY OF TRUSTEES, ETC.   37

(22.) To comply with the award of the arbitrators arising between themselves and other parties, under the school law.

(23.) To provide, at the expense of the section, for the cleaning of the school house and the lighting of fires, &c.

(24.) To provide a well, play yard and separate conveniences for boys and girls.

(25.) To provide an assistant for their school, in case the number of enrolled pupils exceeds fifty.

(26.) To see that the prescribed programme is fully carried out.

(27.) To establish a free public school library as required by law, to see that it is available to the inhabitants, and that it is properly managed.

(28.) To make out an estimate and send it to the township council for the collection of the school rate.

(29.) To take possession and have sole custody of all public school property, movable property, moneys, &c.

(30.) To obtain a legal title to their school premises, as provided by law, and if a conveyance cannot be obtained to register the award of the arbitrators.

(31.) To do whatever they may judge expedient in regard to the building, fitting, &c., of the school house, appendages, play ground, enclosures, lands, and movable property.

(32.) To appoint by written agreement, and fix the amount of the salary of all male and female teachers employed by them. To do this they have sole authority.

(33.) To provide a teacher's residence, where desirable.

(34.) To appoint a secretary-treasurer, &c.

(35.) To establish, if they judge expedient (with the consent of the inspector), two or more schools in their section.

(36.) To obtain from the township assessor the school census of their section once a year.

(37.) To apply to the township council, as required by law, once a year, before the August meeting (except in case of a site and building), to raise any school rate required by them.

NOTE.—The trustees can compel the council to collect the required amount by *mandamus* from one of the divisions of the High Court of Justice, should the council refuse to do so.

(38.) To exempt at their pleasure all indigent persons from section school rates, and provide the children of such persons with text books.

(39.) To sue non-residents for rate bills or school fees. (See section 6, chapter iv.)

4

(40.) To resign the office of trustee (if necessary), with the consent in writing of the co-trustees.

(41.) To decline re-election if they see fit for *four* years next after going out of office.

(42.) To apply to the county council against any objectionable act or by-law of a township council altering the boundaries of the school section, or to request an adjustment of their school section boundaries.

(43.) To comply with the school law and regulations generally.

N.B.—No school meeting of their constituents can deprive trustees of any of these powers, or prevent their exercise.

CHAPTER VI.
PUBLIC SCHOOL MEETINGS.

1.—Day of Annual School Meeting fixed by Law.

The day fixed by statute for the annual school meetings throughout the province is the last Wednesday of December, at ten o'clock in the forenoon. The proceedings cannot close before eleven o'clock, nor be kept open after four o'clock P.M. of that day. They cannot stand over to the following day, nor be adjourned, nor fail, should only four ratepayers be present. (School Act, secs. 15 and 22; see also next section of this chapter.)

NOTE.—If the last Wednesday be a holiday, then the next day will do.

2.—Public Notice of Meeting must be given by Trustees.

Three public notices, to be posted in as many conspicuous places in the school section, should be issued at least six clear days before the day of meeting, and signed by the secretary (by direction of the trustees), or by a majority of the trustees themselves. The corporate seal need not be attached to them. These notices should state the *time* and *place* of meeting, and all the business to be brought forward. Should the meeting fail to be held for want of notice on the part of the trustees, or other cause, any two ratepayers, or the inspector, may call a school meeting. Sch. Act, secs. 40 and 16.*

NOTE.—The foregoing relates to cases in which trustees refuse or neglect to call the annual meeting; but in case of inadvertence, or error, the trustees can at once call the meeting themselves, or authorize their secretary to do so.

---

* Directions how to conduct School Meetings, printed on a large sheet, can be obtained from Messrs. Copp, Clark & Co., Toronto. or other booksellers, for 10 cents.

Forms of Trustees' " Notice of an Annual School Meeting," three on a half-sheet, can be obtained from Messrs. Copp, Clark & Co., Toronto, or other boookseller, for 5 cents. Forms of Notice of Special School Meeting, three on a sheet, can also be obtained for 5 cents. Numerous other School forms are also supplied by them or any bookseller. See list.

3.—Who are, and who are not, School Electors of a Section.

Every school ratepayer of the section, of full age, whether resident or non-resident, who is not a supporter of a separate school (or who is a farmer's son) has a right to be present and vote at a school meeting. (*Ibid*, secs. 14 and 21.)

NOTE.—A ratepayer is defined in the School Act to "mean an assessed householder, owner or tenant, or any person entered on the assessment roll as a farmer's son, or any person assessed for income." (*Ibid*, sec. 2, cl. 7.)

4.—Declaration of School Section Elector's Right to Vote.

In case an objection is made to the right of any person to vote at any such election in any municipality or upon any other subject connected with public school purposes therein, the returning officer, chairman, or other officer presiding at the election or meeting, shall require the person whose right of voting is objected to, to make the following declaration or affirmation :—

"(1) I, A. B., do declare and affirm that I am an assessed ratepayer (or farmer's son, *as the case may be*) in school section ———; (2) that I am a supporter of the public school in said school section No. ———; (3) that I am of the full age of twenty-one years ; (4) that I have the right to vote at this election" [*or* meeting, *as the case may be*].

"Whereupon the person making such declaration shall be permitted to vote." (*Ibid*, sec. 21.)

NOTE.—"Any person convicted of [making a false declaration of his right to vote] upon the complaint of any person, shall be punishable by fine or imprisonment, at the discretion of the Court of General Sessions, or by a penalty of not less than five dollars, or more than ten dollars, to be sued for and recovered with costs before a Justice of the Peace, by the Public School trustees of the city, town, village, school section, or other division, for its use." (*Ibid*. sec. 249. See note to clause (5) sec. 6 of this chapter on the next page.)

5.—Chairman and Secretary of the School Meeting.

The school ratepayers present should elect one of their own number as chairman of the meeting. A secretary should also be appointed. He may be the teacher of the section, or any other competent person. (*Ibid*, sec. 17 ; see also sec. 11 of this chapter, p. 42.)

6.—Duties of the Chairman at a School Meeting.

(1.) To receive nominations for the office of trustee.

(2.) To keep order and to "decide all questions of order, subject to an appeal to the meeting." (Sch. Act, sec. 18.)

(3.) To give a casting vote, but no other. (*Ibid*. sec. 18.)

(4.) To submit all motions to the meeting, in the manner desired by the majority present. (*Ibid*. sec. 18.) (See clause (1) and note to clause (2), section 9 ; and also section 14 of this chapter.)

(5.) To require any elector, whose right to vote is questioned, to make the declaration prescribed by the statute. (See sec. 4 of this chapter.)

NOTE.—The chairman has no right to declare any vote bad unless the voter refuses to make the foregoing declaration ; nor has he any right to receive any protest against the legality of the meeting or its proceedings. Both must be made to the Inspector. (See note to sec. 2, also clause (3) of sec. 9, of this chapter.)

(6.) To hear the verbal declaration of office made (in the words of the statute) by the trustee elect. (Sch. Act, sec. 23.) (See sec. 4 of chap. 1.)

(7.) To transmit to the inspector a copy of the proceedings of the meeting, signed by himself and the secretary, under a penalty of five dollars for neglecting to do so. (*Ibid.* secs. 31 and 254.)

7.—Duties of the Secretary of a School Meeting.

(1.) To make a correct minute of the proceedings.

(2.) If a poll be demanded, to record the votes of the electors in a poll-book.

NOTE.—For mode of taking the votes, in case a poll is demanded, see section 9, clause (2) of this chapter.

(3.) To sign the minutes for transmission to the inspector.

(4.) To hear the declaration of office made by the chairman, in case he should be elected trustee. (*Ibid.* secs. 17, 19 and 23.)

8.—Prescribed Order of Business at a School Meeting.

The following is the order in which the business of an annual school meeting should be taken up. (Sch. Act, sec. 17.) :—

(1.) Calling the meeting to order (by the senior trustee present.)

(2.) Election of chairman and secretary.

(3.) Receiving the trustees' annual report and disposing of the same. (See section 12 of this chapter.)

(4.) Receiving the report of the auditors and disposing of the same.

NOTE.—The school meeting has no legal power to interfere with the trustees in their appointment of the teacher or assistant, or the fixing of his or their salary.

(5.) Electing an auditor for the (next) year.

(6.) Miscellaneous business.

(7.) Electing a trustee or trustees to fill any vacancy or vacancies.

NOTE.—No business can be lawfully transacted at a *special* school meeting, except that for which the meeting was called, unless due notice shall have been given of it by the trustees, inspector, &c., beforehand.

9.—Rules to be observed at each School Meeting.

The following rules should be observed at each school meeting (see also section 10 of this chapter), viz :—

(1.) *Manner of putting motions.*—The names of those who vote for, and of those who vote against a motion may be entered upon the minutes, if required by the majority at the time of voting, and even after the chairman has declared the motion carried.

(2.) " When a poll is demanded by two electors at the meeting for the election of a trustee, the chairman shall forthwith grant the same, and the secretary shall thereupon immediately proceed to record, as herein directed, the names of all qualified electors, who shall present themselves within the time prescribed by this Act, and the secretary shall enter in the pool-book, in separate columns, the names of the candidates proposed and seconded at the nomination, and shall, opposite to such columns, write the names of the electors offering to vote at the election, and shall, in the column on which is entered the name of a candidate voted for by a voter, set the figure ' 1 ' opposite the voter's name, with the residence of the voter." (*Ibid.* sec. 19.)

NOTE.—It is not competent for the chairman to reject any vote tendered. If objection be made to any vote, he should require the person objected to make the declaration given in section 4 of this chapter. The Inspector alone has the right, on complaint made to him, to set aside any vote given.

(3.) *Protest.*—No protest against an election, or other proceedings of the school meeting, shall be received by the chairman. All protests must be sent to the inspector, at least twenty days after the meeting. (*Ibid*, sec. 32.)

NOTE.—An inspector can require "the testimony of witnesses to the truth of facts alleged in any complaint made to him" to be under oath or affirmation. (*Ibid.* sec. 190.)

(4.) *Adjournment.*—A motion to adjourn an annual school meeting before the business is finished, is unlawful; but a motion to adjourn a special school meeting is always in order; provided that such special meeting has not been called for the selection of a school site. (See section 3 of chapter vii.)

(5.) *Reconsidering Motion.*—A motion to reconsider a vote may be made by any elector at the same meeting; but no vote of reconsideration shall be taken more than once on the same question at the same meeting, unless by unanimous consent.

(6.) *Close of the Meeting.*—The school meeting must not close before eleven o'clock in the forenoon, nor shall it continue open after four o'clock in the afternoon—beyond which latter hour no business can be lawfully transacted by the meeting. (Sch. Act, sec. 22.)

(7.) *Transmitting Minutes to Inspector.*—At the close of the meeting the chairman should sign the minutes as entered by the secretary in the minute book, and forthwith send to the inspector a copy of the minutes (as signed by himself and the secretary), under a penalty of five dollars. (*Ibid.* secs. 31 and 254.)

(8.) *Declaration of Office.*—The trustee, or trustees elect, should at once make the declaration of office before the chairman of the meeting, or before a magistrate. In case the chairman is elected trustee, he should in like manner make the declaration of office before the secretary. (*Ibid.* sec. 23.)

NOTE.—In no case is an oath of office, or signed declaration by the trustee elect required. A verbal declaration is sufficient. Even if it be not performed, the trustee is nevertheless a legal trustee until fined by a magistrate for neglect to make the declaration. On being fined, the office is vacated, and a new election should be at once held. Even should a trustee's election be appealed against to the inspector, the trustee himself must hold office and act until his election is legally set aside. The principle is, that an individual coming into office under color of a legal election or appointment, is an officer *de facto* (in fact), and his acts, in relation to the public, are valid until he is lawfully removed, although it be conceded, upon investigation, that his election or appointment was illegal in the first place. When this election is confirmed by the inspector, he becomes a trustee *de jure* (in law) and no further objection can be made to him. (See section 4 of chapter 1.)

10.—Optional Rules.

NOTE.—The following are rules of order suggested, which may or may not be observed, at the pleasure of the meeting, viz :—

(1.) *Addressing Chairman.*—Every elector, previous to speaking, should, unless old or infirm, rise and address himself to the chairman.

(2.) *Order of Speaking.*—When two or more electors rise at once, the chairman shall name the elector who shall speak first, when the other elector, or electors, shall next have the right to address the meeting in order named by the chairman.

(3.) *Motion to be read.*—Each elector may require the question or motion under discussion to be read for his information at any time, but not so as to interrupt an elector who may be speaking.

(4.) *Speaking twice.*—No elector shall speak more than twice on the same question or amendment without leave of the meeting, except in explanation of something which may have been misunderstood, or until every elector choosing to speak, shall have spoken.

(5.) *Motions to be seconded.*—A motion cannot be put from the chair, or debate unless the same be in writing (if required by the chairman), and seconded.

(6.) *Withdrawal of Motion.*—After a motion has been announced, or read by the chairman it shall be deemed to be in the possession of the meeting ; but it may be withdrawn at any time before decision, with the consent of the meeting.

(7.) *Kinds of Motions to be received.*—When a motion is under debate, no other motion shall be received unless to amend it, or to postpone it, or for adjournment, if a special meeting, as provided in clause (4), section 9, of this chapter.

(8.) *Order of putting Motion.*—All questions shall be put in the order in which they are moved. Amendments shall always be put before the main motion ; the last amendment first, and so on.

11.—First Business of the Annual School Meeting.

After appointing a chairman and secretary, the first business of the annual meeting (before electing a new trustee), is (1) the reading of, and deciding upon, the school trustee and auditors' report for the past year; (2) appointment of auditor; (3) miscellaneous business; and (4) the election of trustee or trustees. (School Act, sec. 17. See sec. 8 of this chapter.)

Chap. VI.] PUBLIC SCHOOL MEETINGS. 43

12.—What the Trustees' and Auditors' Report shall contain.

The law declares that the report of the trustees laid before the annual school meeting "shall (1) include a summary of their proceedings; and (2) of the state of the school during the year; together with (3) a full and detailed account of the receipt and expenditure of all school moneys received and expended on behalf of the section for any purpose whatever during the year; which report shall be signed by the trustees, and by either or both of the school auditors of the section." (School Act, sec. 40, cl. 12.) "In case of a difference of opinion between the auditors on any matter in the account, it shall be referred to and decided by the county inspector." (*Ibid.* sec. 39, cl. 2.)

13.—Who may or may not be a Trustee.

Any fit and proper person who is an "actual resident ratepayer within the section, and of the full age of 21 years," may be a trustee thereof; but no inspector, teacher, non-resident, or supporter of a separate school can lawfully hold that office. The chairman of the meeting (if a ratepayer, and otherwise eligible) may be elected. In that case he should make a verbal declaration of office before the secretary of the meeting, or a magistrate. (*Ibid*, secs. 13, 246 and 251. See sec. 4 of chapter i.)

> NOTE.—Should a person elected as trustee refuse to serve, he subjects himself to a penalty of five dollars; but a retiring trustee need not serve for four years after his term of service expires. (See chap. i., secs. 1 and 2.)

14.—Three Modes of Trustee Election prescribed.

In electing a trustee, one of the three modes authorized by custom may be adopted, viz.: (1) by acclamation; (2) by a show of hands; and (3) by polling the votes. The law requires the chairman to adopt the latter mode at the request of any two electors present, even although he may, on a show of hands, have declared the person elected. (*Ibid*, secs. 18 and 19.)

15.—School Election Complaints to be made to Inspector.

Any person having a legal objection, either to the proceedings of the annual meeting, or to the election of the trustee, has a right of appeal against either, within twenty days, to the inspector alone. The inspector is required by law to receive and to investigate the complaint, and either confirm the proceedings and election, or set them aside, in whole or in part, within a reasonable time; his decision is final. (*Ibid*, sec. 32. See sec. 9, cl. 2 of this chapter.)

> NOTE.—Should the inspector require to examine witnesses in any election case or in regard to any other school matter, he can require them to make an affidavit or solemn affirmation before he receives their testimony. (*Ibid*, sec. 194.)
>
> Where certain persons were elected school trustees, and, at a meeting of the board held subsequently to the election, were declared duly elected, but, proceedings having been meanwhile commenced to question the validity of the election,

at a subsequent meeting of the board they acquiesced in the conclusion of the board to hold a new election, and became candidates again, and canvassed as such, until the twenty days allowed for disputing the first election had elapsed (the proceedings formerly commenced for that purpose having been meanwhile dropped), and were not elected at the second election. *Held*, they could not afterwards maintain a suit to have it declared they were the duly elected trustees.—*Foster et al.* v. *Stokes et al.*, 2 O. R., Chy. D., 590.

16.—No Appeal allowed to the Minister of Education.

Should any ratepayer object to the inspector's decision, no appeal is allowed to the head of the Education Department, as Minister Crooks decided (Feb., 1880) that he had "no jurisdiction to review" the decision of the inspector in such matters. (See School Act, sec. 32.)

NOTE.—Should the proceedings and election be set aside, the inspector, or trustees, if directed, should call another meeting for a new election. If no complaint be made to the inspector in writing within twenty days after the meeting, the proceedings (however irregular they may have been) must be held to be valid and binding upon all parties concerned.

17.—Mode of Calling Special School Meetings.

The notice calling a special school meeting should specify the time, place and objects of the meeting. It may be given by the secretary-treasurer or trustees, or by the inspector. Three notices of the meeting should be posted in three or more public places in the section, at least three days before the meeting. (School Act, sec. 40, cl. 1 ; see sec. 2 of this chapter.)

NOTE.—Special school meetings may be held at any convenient place in the day time, or in the evening at 7 or 8 o'clock, provided due notice be given.

18.—What an Ordinary Special School Meeting can do.

A special meeting if called to transact ordinary business, can—

(1.) *Discuss*, and decide at its pleasure, the business named in the notices calling it ; or, it may (unless restricted as below)

(2.) *Adjourn* the further consideration of such business until another time.

(3.) *Rescind* (unless restricted as below) the resolutions of a former meeting, and pass others in their place.

19.—What a School Section Meeting cannot do.

A school meeting cannot lawfully—

(1. *Elections.*)—Rescind any resolution or vote of a former meeting for the election of a school trustee.

(2. *Contract.*)—Rescind any resolution of a former meeting, if in the meantime a contract, agreement or other obligation has been entered into under its authority, unless at the same time it fully provides for the payment of compensation or damages caused by or consequent upon the rescinding of such resolution or vote.

(3.) *Adjourn* the annual school meeting, or any meeting called for the appointment of arbitrators by it and by the trustees to decide upon a school site. (See sec. 4, next chapter.)

(4. *Award.*)—Set aside or ignore the award of arbitrators appointed to select a school site.

NOTE.—By consent of the parties to the reference, an award may be reconsidered. (See section 8 of the next chapter, relating to Arbitration and Awards.)

(5. *Rate Bill.*)—Impose rate bill for fees, fuel, or other purposes upon residents. (See, however, chap. iv., on "Non-residents.")

(6. *Trustees' Rights.*)—Interfere with the trustees in their right to employ a teacher, decide upon the current expenses of the school, or the improvement of the school premises. (See note to sec. 8 of this chapter.)

CHAPTER VII.

SELECTION OF RURAL SCHOOL SITES.

1.—When a School Site requires to be chosen.

There are three cases in which the question of school site comes up for consideration in a school section: (1) on the establishment of a new section; (2) on the change of site in an old section; and (3) on the enlargement of an existing site.

NOTE.—A school site is defined in the Act to mean "such area of land as may be necessary for the school building, teacher's residence, offices and play grounds, connected therewith." (School Act, sec. 2, cl. 4.)

2.—Union of Trustees and Ratepayers in choice of a Site.

Of the three cases relating to the choice of school sites which we have mentioned, the first and second only require the joint action of the trustees and ratepayers; the third is within the province of the trustees alone to determine. (See sec. 10 of this chapter.)

3.—A School Site Meeting cannot Adjourn without action.

The necessity for joint action is clearly obvious, even without an expression of opinion when a new school section first goes into operation. The trustees should therefore call a "special meeting to consider the site proposed." If, at this meeting, a majority of the trustees and a majority of the ratepayers present . . . differ as to the situation of the new site, each party *shall* then and there choose an arbitrator. It is, therefore, not competent for this special meeting to adjourn, in case of a difference of opinion on the subject, until they respectively appoint an arbitrator to select a site for them. (See next section, and sec. 8 of this chapter.)

4.—Failure to call a Meeting, or to appoint an Arbitrator.

In case the trustees refuse to call a special meeting for "procuring" or "changing" a site, the inspector is authorized to do so; or, if at such special meeting a difference of opinion should arise in regard to a site, between the trustees and ratepayers, and the meeting should neglect or refuse to appoint an arbitrator, the law declares that then "it shall be competent for the county inspector, with the arbitrator appointed, to meet and determine the matter; and the inspector, in case of such refusal and neglect, shall have a second or casting vote, provided" he and the one arbitrator appointed should not agree. (School Act, secs. 65 and 68.)

5.—Remedy in case an Arbitrator should refuse to act.

"If only a majority of the arbitrators appointed" to select a site, be "present at any lawful meeting, in consequence of the neglect or the refusal of their colleague to meet them, it shall be competent for those present to make and publish an award upon the matter or matters submitted to them, or to adjourn the meeting for any period not exceeding ten days, and give the absent arbitrator notice of the adjournment." (*Ibid.* sec. 70.)

6.—Power of the Arbitrators.—Kind of Site to be chosen.

The law says, that "in case of a difference as to the choice of a site," the arbitrators appointed "or a majority of them present at any lawful meeting shall have authority to make and publish an award upon the matter or matters submitted to them." Unless, therefore, the choice of one out of two or more sites in dispute is the matter submitted to them, their choice of any site in the section is left free, and they should choose one best adapted to the wants of the section. It should be an acre in size (but cannot be less than half an acre), in a pleasant situation, and (without the consent of the *owner* of the site chosen) should not be within a hundred yards of *his* house, orchard, pleasure-ground or dwelling-house, although it may be close up to the orchard and dwelling-house of any other party. (*Ibid.* secs. 65 and 73.)

> NOTE.—Arbitrators are "entitled to the same remuneration *per diem* and travelling expenses for the time employed" as are county councillors; "and the parties concerned shall pay all the expenses of the arbitration, according to the award of the arbitrators and the school inspector respectively." (*Ibid.* secs. 191 and 72.)

7.—Making and Publishing a written or parol Award.

When the arbitrators have agreed upon their award, they should reduce it to writing, sign and seal it. This is "making" the award. When thus made, it should be sent to the trustees for their information and that of the ratepayers. This is "publishing" it. It is competent, however, for the arbitrators to declare or publish the award orally, in presence of the party concerned, viz., a public meeting of the trustees and ratepayers. Should the award thus published be afterwards, by consent, reduced to writing (as above), it should be identical in its terms with the oral declaration made, that is, it should be merely a written record of it. Any material variation in the written record of the oral award would destroy its validity and finality. (See *Davis* v. *McGivern*, 11 Q. B. R. 112.)

NOTE.—An award may, with the consent, or at the request, of the parties to the reference, be reconsidered. (See sec. 9 of this chapter.)

8.—Summary of General Rules in Regard to Arbitration.

NOTE.—The following are some of the general regulations which govern arbitrations. They are inserted for the guidance and information of the arbitrators.

(1.) *Constitution of the Arbitration Court.*—Any one who can contract can submit matters in dispute to arbitration. Either a friend, or enemy, or a person having an interest in the cause, may be chosen.* Persons unimpeachable on the score of interest or capacity should, if possible, be chosen, and no arbitrator should act as the partisan of the persons appointing him. He should divest himself of all prejudice. If an arbitrator acts corruptly, or with manifest partiality, or colludes with one of the parties, the award is bad. All the arbitrators should be chosen before proceeding to the arbitration, except where otherwise provided (as in the case of a school site.) Notification in writing to the person chosen, and acceptance by him of the office, are necessary to complete the appointment. Where there are an odd number of arbitrators, the majority decide all matters submitted to them, but where the number appointed is two, four, &c., who are equally divided in their opinions, any person who may be selected as umpire has the sole right to determine the points of difference, and make the award. The inspector is *ex officio* and virtually umpire in cases where he and another arbitrator only are present, as he has, in the absence of the third arbitrator, a second or casting vote. In arbitrations under the School Law the directions of the statute should be strictly complied with. Reasonable notice of a meeting must be given to each arbitrator. If one or more be absent, the meeting should be adjourned for about ten days, and notice of another meeting again sent to each arbitrator. At the subsequent meeting, duly notified, two arbitrators can act without their colleague, and make and publish an award.

(2.) *Duties of Arbitrators.*—It is the duty of arbitrators to hear evidence on both sides; one witness may be excluded while the other is being examined. They are the judges of the *admissibility* of evidence, and the competency of the witnesses, as well as of the law and facts of the case. If parties to the arbitration and their witnesses, who are duly notified, do not attend, the arbitrators can proceed *ex parte*, and decide according to the best evidence before them. Where evidence is received, however, it should always be taken in the presence of the

---

* The principle laid down in the Municipal Act should, if possible, be acted upon, viz: "No member, officer or person in the employment of any corporation which is concerned or interested in the arbitration   *   *   *   shall be appointed to act as arbitrator in any case of arbitration under this Act." (Sec. 398, Municipal Act of 1883.)

parties to the reference, or some one attending on their behalf, or after due notice to the parties. Before closing, the arbitrators should receive all the evidence tendered on both sides, and should take notes of it. An arbitrator cannot delegate his power; but, if he obtains the opinion of professional men, he may adopt it as his own. He may, however, delegate purely ministerial acts, such as to go from one place to another, to obtain certain definite information, or estimate the value of some specific work performed; but he cannot direct any person to commit a trespass.

(3.) *Time of making a award.*—If no time be fixed, an award should be made and published within three months from the time of the submission. The time for making an award may, however, be enlarged by the parties to the submission. If time lapses, the power of the arbitrators is gone until it is enlarged.

(4.) *Making and publishing an award.*—If the award be in writing, (as, under the Municipal Act of 1883 (Sec. 405), it must be,) it should be signed in the presence of an attesting witness. Where there are two or more arbitrators, all (or the majority, if all be not present) must execute the award at the same time and place, and in the presence of each other, and an opportunity should be given to the minority, (if disposed) to join or not in the award. An award, however, may be made and published orally. An award is made when the arbitrators have signed it. When so signed by the arbitrators and witnessed, their power is gone, and no single arbitrator can remedy a mistake or correct a blunder. It must be done by the signers, and with the consent of the parties to the reference. An award is published when it is sent to either or both of the parties concerned, or notice is sent to them that it is ready to be delivered. It should be delivered on the day fixed, and then the fees and other expenses on it are payable. 'Any kind of words may be used in an award; but they should be definite, conclusive and final on all points submitted. Arbitrators are not required to give reasons for their award, nor are they answerable for want of skill in performing their duties; but an arbitrator may be called as a witness to prove *facts* which occurred or came under his notice during the reference.

(5.) *Judgment and Experience.*—In *Martin* v. *Kergan* (2 Prac. R. 370), it was held that the parties to an arbitration "have a right to the arguments, experience and judgment of each arbitrator, at every stage of the proceedings."

(6.) *Costs of Arbitration.*—Where the costs of the arbitration are at the discretion of the arbitrators, and the award says nothing about them, each party pays his own costs of reference, and the costs of the award are to be bore equally. (*Glen* v. *Grand Trunk Railway,* 2 Prac R. 377.) Under the School Law the costs may be fixed at the discretion of the arbitrators. The award need not be given up until the amount of costs thus avoided be paid.

(7.) *When an award is bad.*—(1) When it is uncertain and not final. (2) When it contains a mistake on the face of it. (3) When the proceedings are irregular, as from want of notice of meetings, improper conduct of arbitrators in receiving evidence. (4) Corruption or collusion on the part of the arbitrators. (5) Fraud or concealment of material evidence. (6) When the award cannot be acted upon.

(8.) *Arbitration, before award made, may be superseded by natural concurrence.*— Chief Justice Robinson thus laid down the law on this subject:—As a general rule, we take it that where two parties have a difference upon any matter of business, and refer it to arbitration, they may afterwards agree upon the matter on which they had differed, and so may render it unnecessary that any award should be made. By the common law either party might, before the award made, revoke the submission. There have been restrictions lately placed by statute upon this right of one party to revoke without the concurrence of the other, but it would be most unreasonable and inconvenient to hold that both the parties may not come to a settlement of their dispute, and so dispense with the necessity for the arbitrator's proceeding.—*Chief Justice Robinson, in re Vance* v. *King et al, No. 1, Hallowell,* 21 Q. B. R, 187.

(9.) An award in regard to the selection of a school site may be reconsidered. (See the next section of this chapter.)

9.—Power of School Meetings in regard to Awards.

Even after an arbitrator or arbitrators have been appointed to select a site, it is competent for a majority of the trustees and of a public school meeting called for that purpose to agree upon the choice of a site before an award is made. Such an agreement revokes the submission of the matter to arbitrators, who should at once be notified of the fact, so that no award may be made. The school law provides an easy way of meeting the difficulty, should an award be made which is not satisfactory. It provides that "with the consent, or at the request of the parties to the reference, the arbitrators, or a majority of them, shall have authority, within three months from the date of their award, to reconsider such award, and make and publish a second award, which award (or the previous one, if not reconsidered by the arbitrators) shall be binding upon all parties concerned, for at least one year from the date thereof." (School Act, sec. 66.)

10.—Power of the Trustees to Enlarge a School Site.

Where no desire is felt by the trustees or ratepayers to change the site of a section, the trustees have full power to enlarge it at their discretion to an acre or more in extent, and to erect a new school house on it, or to repair or enlarge the old one, without consulting their constituents. (*Ibid.* sec. 74; see secs. 2 and 13 of this chapter.)

11.—Sale or Exchange of the old School Site.

Trustees are required "to dispose by sale or otherwise, of any school site or school property not required by them, in consequence of a change of school site, or other cause, and to convey the same under their corporate seal, and to apply the proceeds thereof for their lawful school purposes." (School Act, sec. 40, cl. 9.)

NOTE.—This case differs materially from one in which a change of boundaries necessitates a change of site. Under such circumstances the law declares that, "In case a school site or school house or other school property *be no longer required*[*] in a section, in consequence of the alteration or the union of school sections, the same shall be disposed of by sale or otherwise, in such manner as a majority of the assessed freeholders and householders in the altered or united school sections may decide at a public meeting called for that purpose." "The inhabitants transferred from one school section to another shall be entitled, for the public school purposes of the section to which they are attached, to such a proportion of the proceeds of the sale of such school house or other public school property, [after, of course, paying the debts of the section,] as the assessed value of their property bears to that of the other inhabitants of the school section from which they have been so separated; and the residue of such proceeds shall be applied to the erection of a new school house in the old school section, or to other public school purposes of such old school section. In the case of united sections,

---

[*] A full explanation of the phrase "no longer required" here used, will be found in Part II. of these Lectures, chap. iii., sec. 11.

the proceeds of the sale shall be applied to the like public school purposes of such united sections." (*Ibid.* sec. 84.)

12.—Owner of Land must Sell School Sites selected.

If the owner of a newly selected school site, or of land adjoining an old site (which the trustees have decided to enlarge), should refuse to sell it, or should ask an unreasonable price for it, the law requires the trustees and owners each to appoint an arbitrator to appraise the damages, to the owner, of such compulsory sale. Upon the tender of payment of these damages to the owner of the land by the trustees, they can take possession of the land for school purposes, and proceed to erect a school house on it, or to enclose it. .(*Ibid.* secs. 68 and 69.)

NOTE.—The School Act defines an owner to "include a mortgagee, lessee or tenant, or other person entitled to a limited interest, and whose claims may be dealt with by arbitration as herein provided." (Sec. 2, cl. 5.)

13.—Privileges of the Owner only relate to a New Site.

On the selection of a person's land for a new school site (with or without his knowledge), within one hundred yards of his garden, orchard, pleasure-ground, or dwelling-house, the owner may either consent to the sale of the new site at a reasonable rate, or he may refuse to sell it, at his pleasure ; but he cannot be compelled to sell it. In regard to the *enlargement* of the old school site, however, the law gives the owner of the chosen land only a restricted privilege, should the trustees offer to buy it. But they can compel a sale when the proposed enlargement is not "made in the *direction* of the orchard, garden, or dwelling-house," provided that it cannot be otherwise enlarged. Without the consent of the owner no part of the garden or grounds attached to the house can be taken. In case of refusal to sell it (within these restrictions), the law requires the trustees and owner, each, to appoint an arbitrator to appraise the damages, and upon tender by the trustees of the amount of damages awarded, the trustees can take possession and use the land for the purposes of their trust. (*Ibid.* secs. 73 and 74.)

NOTE.—The provisions of the law on the compulsory sale of school sites are twofold, although they have been frequently confounded together. Sections of the 67th section refer first to "land selected for a new school site," and section 74 to the selection of land for enlarging existing school premises. In these two cases, the trustees can demand an arbitration should the owner of the selected or enlarged site refuse to sell, or ask too large a price for the land. In the first class of cases, (*i.e.*, the selection of a *new* site,) the owner can lawfully refuse to sell, or to submit to arbitration, when the site selected is within 100 yards of *his* "orchard, garden, pleasure-ground or dwelling-house ;" but where the trustees merely wish to enlarge their existing school premises, the owner has only a restricted right, (as explained above,) which shall not "be held to restrict trustees in the enlargement of a school site existing to the required dimensions." (Sec. 74.) The provision of the law does not in any case apply to other persons whose house, orchard, &c., may happen to be within 100 yards of the proposed site, and who are not in any way concerned in the sale of land for the enlarged site. (S. 73.)

14.—Township Councils may Purchase School Sites.

The Municipal Institutions Act authorizes township councils to pass by-laws "for obtaining such real property as may be required for the erection of public school houses thereon, and for other public school purposes, and for the disposal thereof when no longer required," etc. (Sec. 490, cl. 7, of the Act of 1883.)

15.—Decisions of the Courts in regard to School Sites.

(1.) *In selecting a Site, Trustees cannot act without consulting their constituents.*—The Court of Queen's Bench has decided that the trustees cannot, without reference to the [assessed] freeholders and householders of the section, determine upon a site for the school house, and impose a rate to meet the expense of its purchase.—*Orr v. Ranney et al, No. 15, Westminster.* 12 Q. B. R. 377.

(2.) *Arbitration before award made may be superseded by mutual concurrence.*—Chief Justice Robinson thus laid down the law on this subject:—As a general rule, we take it that where two parties have a difference upon any matter of business, and refer it to arbitration, they may afterwards agree upon the matter on which they had differed, and so may render it unnecessary that any award should be made. By the common law either party might, before the award made, revoke the submission. There have been restrictions lately placed by statute upon this right of one party to revoke without the concurrence of the other, but it would be most unreasonable and inconvenient to hold that both the parties may not come to a settlement of their dispute, and so dispense with the necessity for the arbitrators proceeding.—*Chief Justice Robinson, in re Vance v. King et al, No. 1, Hallowell.* 22 Q. B. R. 187.

(3.) *First arbitration in regard to a School Site cannot be set aside by a subsequent Special Meeting.*—The Court of Common Pleas has decided the following case: When a meeting was held to change the site of a school house, and arbitrators appointed, who met and decided the question, but their decision was not acted upon; subsequently another meeting was called, and their decision and proceedings were acted upon and the site changed. *Held*, that the proceedings were irregular, and that the trustees had no authority to change the site of the school house without the sanction of a special meeting of the [assessed] freeholders and householders, and that the second meeting had no authority to alter the determinations previously made.—*Williams v. Trustees, No. 8, Plympton.* 7 C. P. R. 559.

(4.) *Replevin—Arbitration in regard to School Site. Blanks filled in after execution—Award rendered invalid thereby.*—The Court of Common Pleas decided the following case: Replevin.*—Two defendants avowed [i.e., maintained and justified the act done by them]; the third pleaded the convening of a special meeting of freeholders and householders of a certain school section to procure a school site, when it was agreed to procure a certain piece of ground and erect a school house thereon, which was done. That plaintiff was a resident freeholder when the meeting was held and when his goods were seized, and was assessed $80 for building said school, &c. The plaintiff pleaded that the meeting above set forth was null and void, because before the said meeting another had been convened according to law, when a difference of opinion existed between a majority of the freeholders and householders as to choosing a school site, and arbitrators were appointed, who decided upon a certain site, which decision remains in force, and the defendants in contravention thereof wrongfully purchased the site men oned in their plea, and wrongfully distrained, &c. Upon demurrer, *Held*, that the second meeting pleaded by the defendant was a violation of the provisions of the statute,

---

**Replevin: the name of an action for the recovery of goods and chattels. *A party*: to re-deliver goods which have been distrained, to the original possessor of them, on his giving pledges in an action of replevin.

and that the plaintiff was entitled to judgment. The arbitrators to whom a reference in this cause was made under the School Act, executed an award, the description of the lot not being fully inserted, but a blank being left therefor, which was afterwards filled in and the word lot altered into gore. *Held*, that the award was insufficient. *Held*, also, that school trustees who executed a warrant as such trustees under the seal of the trustee corporation, were not personally responsible. —*Ryland* v. *King et al, No. 1, Hallowell*. [See decision of the Queen's Bench below, in effect reversing this case.] 12 C. P. R. 198. For definition of the word "*replevin*" see * below.

(5.) *A similar case decided by the Court of Queen's Bench.*—Replevin against two school trustees and one King, a bailiff, for a horse. Defendants pleaded, 1, That they did not take; and 2, an avowry, setting out in substance that on the 30th of October, 1858, a special meeting of the freeholders and householders of the section had been duly called to procure a school site and erect a school house thereon, at which it was agreed to procure a certain site named : that this was procured and the school house built : that the plaintiff was duly assessed for a sum specified : that the trustees by their warrant commanded King to collect it ; and that after demand and default made he seized the horse. The plaintiff pleaded to the avowry, 1st, *de injuriá* ; and, 2nd, as to the justification by the trustees, that the meeting was void, because before it took place a special meeting of the freeholders was duly held to procure a school site, at which a majority of the trustees differed from a majority of those present with regard to the site, in consequence of which the freeholders and householders, the trustees and local superintendent, each appointed an arbitrator to decide the question ; that the arbitrators determined upon a site specified, different from that mentioned in the avowry, which award remained in force ; and that the trustees, contrary to this decision, wrongfully purchased the site mentioned in the avowry. The defendants replied that there was no such award. As to this issue taken upon the first plea of the defendants, it appeared that the horse was seized by King under a warrant signed by two trustees, commencing : "We, the undersigned trustees of school section," &c., and sealed with the corporate seal. *Held*, that the trustees were liable personally, not in their corporate capacities only. With regard to the second and third issues, raised by the plea of *de injuriá* to the avowry, and replication denying the award, the evidence showed that in 1857 the inhabitants were divided as to the choice of a school site, and an award was made but not acted upon : that in 1858 the same difference existed, and one of the trustees also differed from his co-trustees ; that in March the two trustees, defendants, obtained a conveyance of half an acre, part of lot 15, and in May a meeting was held at which arbitrators were named and an award made ; but the inhabitants being still dissatisfied, another meeting was held in July, when the arbitrators mentioned in the plea to the avowry were chosen. In the meantime the building was commenced upon the land conveyed. On the 4th of September an award was drawn up [in which a blank was left for a description of the site]. On the 30th of October, 1858, a meeting was held, having been regularly called by the two trustees, to settle the question finally, and a resolution passed adopting [as the site] the land conveyed. In April, 1859, the two trustees, defendants, met, the third being absent from the country, and resolved upon the rate, which was inserted by the clerk in the roll, and the warrant was issued to King, who seized the plaintiff's horse. The plaintiff, after that, set about getting the award of September, 1858, which was afterwards filled up by two of the arbitrators, who stated that it had been left blank because they did not know the precise description of London's land. *Held*, that upon the second issue raised by plaintiff, defendants were entitled to succeed, for the evidence sustained the avowry. And that upon the third issue raised by the plaintiff they were also entitled to the verdict, for there

---

* *Replevin:* the name of an action for the recovery of goods and chattels. *Replevy:* to re-deliver goods which have been distrained, to the original possessor of them, on his giving pledges in an action of replevin.

was in fact no award made, and even as it was altered after execution the description was too uncertain. Ryland v. The same defendants, in the Court of Common Pleas, commented upon. [See above.] *Held*, that under the circumstances proved, the reference did not make the subsequent meeting illegal. *Held*, also, upon demurrer, that the avowry was good, the omission of any averment essential to the validity of the rate being cured by the second plea of the plaintiff to it, which relied wholly upon the award: that the second plea of the plaintiff was bad, for not showing that before the award the trustees and inhabitants had not duly selected the site built upon, as they might do notwithstanding the reference; and that the replication to it denying the award was a good answer. *Vance* v. *King et al, No. 1, Hallowell.* 21 Q. B. R. 187.

(6.) *Site wrongfully conveyed—Claim.*—The Court of Chancery decided the following case: "A school site had been granted to certain parties in trust, and a school-house erected thereon, but by mistake the wrong site was conveyed. The grantor subsequently made a mortgage on his estate, but exempted the portion reserved for a school site. He died shortly afterwards, leaving his son and heir-at-law a minor. The defendant, during the minority of the heir, obtained a lease of the premises, excepting the site in question; but on the coming of age of the heir obtained a deed from the said heir, without any reservation of the school site. About the same time, or a little before, he also obtained an assignment of the mortgage so as to perfect his title. He then claimed the land on which the school-house was erected, on the ground that in consequence of the mistake no title was vested in the trustees, whereupon the trustees of the school section filed a bill against him, and it was *held*, that he had express notice of the trustees' title; and that even if the trustees were volunteers as to this piece of land, the defendant was also a volunteer, and being prior to him they had a right to the aid of equity to have his title to said piece of land cancelled, or a conveyance thereof from said defendant. *Held* also, that the township council was a necessary party to the suit."—*School Trustees* v. *Farrell*, 5 L. J. 230, Chy.

(7.) *School reserve binding.*—The Court of Chancery has decided the following case: "A reservation for school purposes is of such a character as to be the subject of dedication. The owners of land in 1856 caused the same to be surveyed and laid off into village lots, and on the plan thereof which was duly registered, marked a portion as 'reserve for school ground.' An auction sale of lots took place during the same month with reference to the lots not fronting on the reserve, when lots to the value of $20,000 were sold; and after the auction lots were sold privately, according to the plan. The school trustees did not take possession of the school reserve. Subsequently conveyances were executed to S. of all the undisposed of portion of the town as surveyed. S. in January, 1863, caused a new plan to be prepared and registered, in which the school reserve was laid out into village lots, some of which had meanwhile been bought by the defentant from an intermediate owner, with notice of the original plan and the reservation for school purposes. *Held*, on a bill filed in 1876, that the original plan was binding; that the conveyance to S. did not give him the ownership of the soil of the streets or reserves for public purposes; and that the defendant was not entitled under the 36 Vic. c. 22, Ont., to be paid for any improvements he had made upon the lots forming part of the school reserve."—*The Corporation of Wyoming and the Public School Board of Wyoming* v. *Bell*, 24 Chy. 564.

(8.) *Actions against Trustees in regard to School Sites.*—A school trustee, by desire of the board, attended an auction and bought for the board a piece of property for a school site, and he signed the contract with his own name only. The board afterwards, by several resolutions, during three years, unanimously recognized the purchase as their own, and paid three installments of the purchase money. In an estimate under the corporate seal, the board applied to the town council for money to pay "for school premises for a central school, contracted for and agreed to be paid, $1,570; for building a central school-house on said purchased premises, $7,180." It was shewn that there was no other property or contract to which this language could refer than the property or contract mentioned. The town council did not comply with the requisition, and ultimately trustees were elected a majority of whom determined to repudiate the purchase. *Held*, in a suit against the board by the purchaser for indemnification in respect of the remainder of the purchase money, that the plaintiff was entitled to relief.—*Smith* v. *The School Trustees of Belleville*, 16 Chy. 130.

(9.) *Dissent of School Trustees in regard to Sites*.—A dissent by school trustees from a decision of the ratepayers as to a site for the school, should be intimated promptly, and if not announced till after the expiration of the current year, it is too late.—*Coupland* v. *The School Trustees of Nottawasaga*, 15 Chy. 339.

(10.) *Formation and Alteration of School Sections—Notice to Ratepayers.*—*Held*, Draper, J., diss., that the request of the freeholders and householders and householders mentioned in 13 and 14 Vict., c. 48, s. 18, sub. s, 4, applies only to the union of two or more sections into one; and that the municipality of a township may pass a by-law to bring back exclusively within their own jurisdiction any part which has been united with a school section in another township, and may alter and arrange the sections within their own township; provided only that all parties affected by such intended alteration shall appear to have been duly notified. By a resolution of the district council in 1849 a union school section was formed, consisting of part of what had formerly been section ten in Saltfleet and part of section three in Barton. In 1854 a by-law was passed by the municipality of Saltfleet, which defined the limits of section ten and brought it entirely within Saltfleet, excluding that part of Barton which had belonged to it. *Held*, that a ratepayer of Barton could not object that no notice had been given to those affected in Saltfleet; and *Semble*, per Robinson, C. J., that no notice was required to those in Barton. It is not necessary to recite in such by-law that the requisite notice, &c., have been given. *In re Ness and the Municipality of Saltfleet*, 13 Q. B. 408. See, also, *Morrison and the Municipality of Arthur*, Ib. 279, which is overruled by this decision.

NOTE.—See also decisions of the Superior Courts in regard to School Houses, chapter ii, section 13, page 19; also decisions as to Trustees' personal responsibility, chapter I, section 10, page 11

CHAPTER VIII.

COMPULSORY ATTENDANCE OF ABSENTEE CHILDREN.

1.—Right of every Child to receive an Education.

The public school law requires the parent or guardian of "every" child, from the age of seven to twelve years to cause such child to attend some school, or be otherwise educated, for one hundred days in every year;* and otherwise such parent or guardian shall be subject

* While the school law thus declares the right of every child to attend school and receive an education therein, *(or otherwise)* it also very properly makes it the imperative *duty* of trustees to provide in their school house sufficient "accommodation" or room for the attendance of every child of school age in the section, at the rate of nine square feet of space on the floor for each child. (see chap. ii, sec. 9, page 17.)

*The form to be used in taking the school census will be furnished by Messrs. Copp, Clark & Co., Toronto, or by any other bookseller, free by post for 5 cts.

to the penalties provided by the School Act. (Sch. Act, secs. 210 and 214.)

NOTE.—The provision of the Act does not require any Roman Catholic to attend a public school, or a Protestant to attend a Roman Catholic separate school. (*Ibid.* sec. 216.)

2.—Duty of School Trustees in this matter.

(1.) The law authorizes the trustees of every rural public school to appoint an officer who shall notify personally, or by letter or otherwise, the parents or guardians of such children of the neglect or violation on their part of the provisions of the law and the consequences thereof. (*Ibid.* sec. 213.)

NOTE.—In order to enable the masters to perform their duty in this matter the law requires the township clerks to furnish annually their secretary-treasurer with the names of parents and the number of children between the ages of 5 and 13 in their school sections. (*Ibid.* sec. 115.)

(2.) In case, after having been so notified, the parents or guardians of such children continue to neglect or violate the provisions of this Act, it shall be the duty of the trustees to impose a rate-bill on such parents or guardians not exceeding one dollar per month for each of their children not attending school; or

(3.) To make complaint of such neglect or violation to a magistrate having jurisdiction in such cases, unless they are satisfied that such neglect or violation has not been wilful, or caused by poverty, ill-health, or too great distance from school. (*Ibid.* secs. 214 and 219.)

3.—Power and Duty of the Police and other Magistrate.

(1.) It shall be competent for such magistrate to investigate and decide upon any complaint made by the trustees, or by any person authorized by them against any parent or guardian for the violation of the Act, and to impose a fine not exceeding *five* dollars for the first wilful offence, and double that penalty for every subsequent offence. (*Ibid.* sec. 218.)

(2.) The magistrate shall not be bound to, but may, in his discretion, forego to issue the warrant for the imprisonment of the offender, as in said section is provided. (*Ibid.* cl. 2.)

(3.) It shall be the duty of such magistrate to ascertain, as far as may be, the circumstances of any party complained of for not sending his child or children to some school, or otherwise educating him or them, and being satisfied that the mission is not wilful, the magistrate shall not award punishment, but shall report the circumstances to the trustees of the school section or division in which the offence has occurred. (*Ibid.* sec. 219.)

NOTE.—It will be seen from these sections of the Act that school trustees are made responsible for carrying out the "compulsory" sections of the Act quoted.

Should they neglect to impose the required rate bill, as provided, or to duly report every case of delinquency to the magistrate, they become personally responsible for the amount of the rate bill or of the fine which may be lost to the section or division in consequence of such neglect on their part. Besides, they are responsible for the loss of the apportionment which would have been made on the average attendance of the absentees.

CHAPTER IX.

PUBLIC SCHOOL TEACHERS.

1.—Who are qualified Public School Teachers.

A duly qualified public school teacher is one who, at the time of engaging with the trustees, and during the period of such engagement, holds "a legal certificate of qualification." (Sch. Act, sec. 153.)

NOTE.—One of the Superior Courts has decided that trustees cannot legally apply a rate to the payment of a teacher who does not possess the necessary qualifications as such, under the school laws. (See clause 4, sec. 11 of this chap., p. 63.)

2.—Who cannot hold the office of Public School Teacher.

No high or public school trustee, and no inspector, can lawfully hold the office of, or act as, a public school teacher, and *vice versa*. (Sch. Act, sec. 240.)

3.—Assistant Teachers in a Public School.

Whenever the number of pupils enrolled in a public school exceeds *fifty* there should be a teacher and an assistant, and, at the option of the trustees, a monitor. A monitor cannot take the place of an "assistant teacher," or be put in charge of a division of the school. He can only aid the master or assistant in the classes. (See Regulations.)

4.—Agreements between Trustees and Teachers.

"All agreements between trustees and teachers, to be valid and binding, shall be in writing, signed by the parties thereto, and sealed with the corporate seal of the trustees," and "may lawfully include any stipulation to provide the teacher with board and lodging." (Sch. Act, sec. 152.) Payment may also be made quarterly or monthly.

NOTE.—All agreements between trustees and a teacher, to be valid, must be authorized at a regular or special meeting of the trustees, and must be signed by at least two of the trustees and the teacher; they must also have the *corporate seal* of the section attached to them (as above), otherwise the trustees may be made *personally responsible* for the fulfilment of such agreements, and can be sued on them individually by the teacher. It should also be entered in the trustees' book, and a copy of it given to the teacher.* The trustees being a corporation, their agreement with their teacher is binding on their successors in office, if made in accordance with the foregoing section; and should they refuse or wilfully neglect to exercise the corporate powers vested in them to give it effect, they would be personally liable for the amount due a teacher. The mode of settling disputes between trustees and a teacher is by suit in the Division Court. (School Act, secs. 156 and 157.)

NOTE.—See "Decisions of the Courts relating to Trustees and Teachers," section 11 of this chapter, page 63.

5.—General powers of the Master of a Public School.

In every school in which there are two or more teachers employed therein, the trustees shall determine who shall be considered as the master of the school.

NOTE.—The head teacher employed in any public school in which there is more than one teacher, shall be designated and known as the *master ;* and the others shall be named first, second or third, &c., assistant *teacher*.

The master of every school is a public officer, and, as such, shall have power, and it shall be his duty to observe and enforce the following rules, sanctioned by the Department. All special rules of the school not authorized in the Official Regulations, which may be adopted in a school, must first have the sanction of the trustees before they can be lawfully enforced by the teacher.

NOTE.—Neglect of the foregoing, in many cases, involves the teacher in unnecessary trouble and litigation. He is merely an officer or agent of the trustees, and possesses no powers, except those conferred upon him by statute, Departmental regulations, or by the trustees themselves. All rules, therefore, which he enforces should have the sanction of law, regulation, or the authority of the trustees.

(1.) *See that the Rules are observed.*—He shall see that the general rules and regulations, and any special rules (not inconsistent with them) which may be approved by the trustees for their respective schools, are duly and faithfully carried out, subject to appeal, in case of dissatisfaction, to the inspector.

NOTE.—The master is required to read, or cause to be read, in his school, at least once in each quarter, (or otherwise inform the pupils of,) so much of the regulations as shall be necessary to give them a proper understanding of the rules by which they are governed.

(2.) *Prescribe Duties of Teachers.*—He shall prescribe (with the assent of the trustees) the duties of the several teachers in his school, but he shall be responsible for the control and management of the classes under their charge.

---

* Forms of agreement between trustees and teacher, can be obtained from Messrs. Copp, Clark & Co., Front Street, Toronto, or any bookseller, free by post, for 5 cents.

(3.) *Religious Exercises—Ten Commandments.*—He shall see that the regulations in regard to *Opening and Closing Exercises of the Day* are observed, and that the Ten Commandments are duly taught to all the pupils, and repeated by them once a week.

6.—Discipline in the School—Authority over Pupils.

It shall also be the duty of each master and teacher of a public school, to observe the following regulations :—

(1.) *General Principles of Government.*—Masters and teachers are to evince a regard for the improvement and general welfare of their pupils; treat them with kindness, combined with firmness, and aim at governing them by their affections and reason, rather than by harshness and severity. Teachers shall also, as far as practicable, exercise a general care over their pupils in and out of school, and shall not confine their instructions and superintendence to the usual school duties, but shall, as far as possible, extend the same to the mental and moral training of such pupils, to their personal deportment, to the practice of correct habits and good manners among them, and should omit no opportunity of inculcating the principles of TRUTH and HONESTY, the duty of respect to superiors, and obedience to all persons placed in authority over them.

(2.) *Discipline.*—Each master and teacher shall practice such discipline in his school class or department, as would be exercised by a kind, firm and judicious parent in his family. It is strictly enjoined upon all teachers in the schools to avoid the appearance of indiscreet haste in the discipline of their pupils; and in any difficult cases which may occur, to apply to the master, [if an assistant,] inspector, or to the trustees, (as the case may be,) for advice and direction.

NOTE.—The following are modes to be adopted or avoided :

(1.) *Proper.*—Reproof, kindly but firmly given, either in private or before the school, as circumstances require it, or such severe punishment as the case really warrants, administered as directed in the above regulation.

(2.) *Improper.*—Contemptuous language, reproof administered in passion, personal indignity or torture, and violation of the laws of health.

(3.) *State of feeling among Pupils.*—Masters and teachers shall cultivate kindly and affectionate feelings among the pupils; discountenance quarrelling, cruelty to animals, and every approach to vice.

(4.) *Power to suspend Pupils.*—The master shall suspend (subject to an appeal by the parent or guardian to the trustees) any pupil for any of the following reasons :—

(*a*) Truancy persisted in.
(*b*) Violent opposition to authority.
(*c*) Repetition of any offence after notice.

(d) Habitual and determined neglect of duty.
(e) The use of profane, or other improper language.
(f) General bad conduct, and bad example, to the injury of the school.

(g) Cutting, marring, destroying, defacing or injuring any of the public school property, such as buildings, furniture, seats, fences, trees, shrubbery, &c., or writing any obscene or improper words on the fences, walls, privies, or any part of the premises. Any master suspending a pupil for any of the causes above named, shall, immediately after such suspension, give notice thereof, in writing, to the parent or guardian of such pupil, and to the trustees, in which notice shall be stated the reason for such suspension; but no pupil shall be expelled without the authority of the trustees.

(5.) *Expulsion of Pupils.*—When the example of any pupil is very hurtful to the school, and in all cases where reformation appears hopeless, it shall be the duty of the master, with the approbation of the trustees, to expel such pupil from the school. But any pupil under public censure, who shall express to the master his regret for such a course of conduct, as openly and explicitly as the case may require, shall, with the approbation of the trustees and master, be re-admitted to the school.

NOTE.—The School Law declares that "any pupil who shall be adjudged so refractory by the trustees (or a majority of them) and the teacher, that his presence in school is deemed injurious to the other pupils, may be dismissed from such school, and where practicable, removed to an Industrial school." (Sec. 40, cl. [8].)

NOTE.—The master, under clause (2) of section 5 of this chapter, may authorize the assistant to suspend or otherwise deal with pupils in his class, as provided in clause (4) of this section.

7.—Duties of Masters and Teachers in regard to Teaching.

The law requires each master or teacher of a public school:

(1.) "*To Teach Diligently* and faithfully all the branches required to be taught in the school, according to the terms of his engagement with the trustees, and according to the provisions of the School Act, and the regulations of the Education Department. (Sch. Act, sec. 154, [1].)

(2.) *Classify Pupils.*—He shall classify the children according to the books used; study those books himself, and teach according to the improved method recommended in their prefaces. The division of the pupils into classes, as prescribed by the programme, shall be strictly observed; and no teacher shall be allowed to take his or her class beyond the limits fixed for the classes taught by such teachers, without the consent of the master (if an assistant) or inspector, except for occasional reviews; but individual pupils, on being qualified, may, with the consent of the master, be advanced from a lower to the higher class.

(3.) *Constant employment to Pupils.*—He shall give the children under his charge constant employment in the studies prescribed in the authorized programme; and endeavour by judicious and diversified modes to render the exercises of the school pleasant as well as profitable. In giving out the lessons for the next day, difficult parts should be explained, and where necessary, the best mode of studying them should be pointed out to the pupils.

NOTE.—The object of the school programme is two-fold—to provide work, (1), for the master or teacher, and (2), for the pupils while he is engaged. No master is required to teach more than 27½ hours per week; but while he is teaching one class one subject, the other classes should be engaged in studying the other subjects, according to the programme.

(4.) *Time Table.*—Each master shall keep, in some conspicuous place in the school-room, a time-table, showing the order of exercises for each day in the week, and the time for each exercise, as prescribed in the programme of studies for public schools.

(5.) *Registers—Prizes.*—The pupils' names should be carefully entered in the general, entrance, and daily class and other registers. Should prizes be given merit alone should determine who are entitled to receive them. (See School Act, sec. 154, cl. [2].)

(6.) *Term Examination*—Each class in every school shall be open for public examination and inspection during the last week of every term; and the master or teacher shall call upon every pupil in the school, unless excused, to review or recite in the course of such examination. (*Ibid*, cl. [8].)

NOTE.—See clause (1) of section 13 of this chapter.

(7.) *In School at 8¾ a.m., &c.*—All teachers shall be in their respective schools, and open their rooms for reception of pupils, at least fifteen minutes in the morning and five minutes in the afternoon before the specified time for beginning school; and during school hours they shall faithfully devote themselves to the duties of their office.

8.—Duties of Teachers in regard to School Premises.

(1.) *Care of School Property.*—Each master or teacher shall exercise the strictest vigilance over the public school property in his charge—the building, outhouses, fences, &c., furniture, apparatus, and books belonging to the school, so that they may receive no injury; and give prompt notice, in writing, to the trustees or person appointed by them, under chapter ii, section 12, (if in cities, towns or villages, to the inspector,) of any repairs which may require to be made to the building, premises, or furniture, &c., and of any furniture or supplies which may be required for the school.

(2.) *Regulations in regard to School Premises, &c.*—The trustees having made such provision relative to the school-house and its appendages as required by law (see section 9, chapter ii), it shall be the duty of the master to give strict attention to the proper ventilation and temperature, as well as to the cleanliness of the school-house; he shall also prescribe such rules for the use of the yard and out-buildings connected with the school-house as will insure their being kept in a neat and proper condition; and he shall be held responsible for any want of cleanliness about the premises.

(3.) *School open for Pupils.*—Care must be taken to have the school-house ready for the reception of pupils at least *fifteen* minutes before the time prescribed for opening the school, in order to afford shelter to those who may arrive before the appointed hour. (See clause (7), section 7 of this chapter.)

(4.) *Out-Premises.*—The master or teacher shall see that the yards, sheds, privies, and other out-buildings are kept in order, and that the school house and buildings are locked at all proper times; and that all deposits of sweepings from rooms or yards are removed from the premises.

(5.) *Fires and Sweeping.*—He shall employ, at a compensation to be fixed by the trustees, a suitable person to make fires, to sweep the rooms and halls daily, and dust the windows, walls, seats, desks, and other furniture in the same; but no master, assistant teacher, or pupil shall be required to perform such duty, unless voluntarily, and with suitable compensation.

9.—Duties of Teachers in regard to Library, Reports, &c.

(1.) *Act as Librarian.*—Each master or teacher shall act as librarian of the school, and take charge of the books; also make, keep, and preserve a catalogue of the same; deliver, charge, receive, and credit the volumes given out, and keep a register of the same; number, label, and catalogue the books; and make returns of the library, its books, &c, as required by the library regulations.

(2.) *The Library.*—He shall keep the library open for the distribution and return of books to the scholars and ratepayers of the school division, on Friday afternoon of each week; but this duty shall not be permitted to interfere with the regular exercises of the school.

(3.) *General Register.*—He shall keep a general register of the school (to be furnished at the expense of the trustees), in which shall be entered, in each term, the date of the admission of each pupil; the names of the pupils in each of the classes in the school; the promotion of pupils; date of a pupil's leaving the school, and destination, both as to place and occupation; and such other information as shall at all times give a correct idea of the condition of the school.

(4.) *Daily Register.*—He shall also keep the daily register (provided at the expense of the trustees), in which shall be entered the names and daily attendance of pupils, their proficiency in various studies, and other information.

NOTE.—See clause 5 of section 7 and (3), of section 13 of this chapter.

(5.) *Returns.*—The master [or teacher] shall make such returns, and at such times, as may be required by the [master] inspector, or trustees, relating to his class, school, or department.

(6.) *Reports.*—He shall make the necessary term special, or annual reports to, and with, the trustees, to the inspector at such times and in such manner as may be required. [See School Act, sec. 154, cl. (10).]

NOTE.—See section 21 of chapter ii. (page 23), and clause (4) of section 12 of this chapter, page 66.

10.—Regulations in regard to Sickness, Visiting Schools, Visitors, Presents, Teachers' Meetings, &c.

(1.) *Absence and Sickness*—No master or teacher shall be absent from the school in which he or she may be employed, without permission of the trustees or inspector, except in case of sickness, in which case the absence of such teacher shall be immediately reported to the trustees; and no deduction from the salary of a teacher shall be made on account of sickness, (not exceeding at the rate of four weeks for the whole year,) as certified by a medical man. (School Act, sec. 158.)

NOTE.—See latter part of section 15, of this chapter.

(2.) *Visiting Schools.*—The inspector may permit a public school master, or teacher, to be absent two of the ordinary teaching days in each half year, for the purpose of visiting and observing the methods of classification, teaching, and discipline practised in other schools than that in which he or she teaches.

NOTE.—This visit, with the name of the school or schools visited, is to be duly reported by such master or teacher to the inspector. Each public school master and teacher must give at least three days' notice of each visit to the trustees. In order that no loss of apportionment may accrue to any school in consequence of the master's absence under this regulation, a proportionate amount of average attendance will be credited to the school for the time so employed by the teacher; but under no circumstances can lost time be lawfully made up by teaching on any of the prescribed vacations, holidays, or half holidays, nor will such time be allowed by the Department, or be reckoned by the inspector; but such permission shall not be given by the inspector if the absence of the teacher will, in his judgment, be injurious to the interests of the school; nor shall this permission be granted to any master or teacher who fails to report, or who has employed the time heretofore given to him otherwise than in visiting schools, as authorized by this regulation.

(3.) *Visitors' Book.*—The master (or teacher) shall keep the visitors book (which is required by law to be furnished by the trustees), in which shall be entered the dates of visits and names of visitors, with such remarks as they may choose to make. The book is to be handed to the visitors for this purpose. [See School Act, sec. 154, cl. (4).]

(4.) *Visitors.*—Each master or trustee shall receive courteously the visitors appointed by law, and afford them every facility for inspecting the books used, and examine into the state of the school; he shall keep the visitors' book accessible, that the visitors may, if they choose, enter remarks in it. The frequency of visits to the school by intelligent persons, animates the pupils, and greatly encourages the faithful teacher.

NOTE.—See clause (2) of section 12 of this chapter.

(5.) *Subscriptions, Collections, Presents, &c.*—No collection shall be taken up, or subscriptions solicited for any purpose, or notice of shows or exhibitions given in any public school, without the consent of the trustees.

NOTE.—No master or teacher shall act as agent for any bookseller or other person, to sell, or in any way promote the sale, for such bookseller or person, of any school library, prize or task book, map, chart, school apparatus, furniture, or stationery; nor receive compensation or equivalent for such sale, or for the promotion of such sale, in any way whatsoever; nor receive presents (unless presented to them on leaving the school), nor award, without the permission of the trustees, medals or other prizes of their own to the pupils under their charge. (School Act, sec. 267.)

(6.) *Teachers' Meetings.*—All masters and teachers in cities, towns and villages, shall regularly attend the teachers' meetings, at such times, and under such regulations, as the inspector shall direct, and by study, recitations and general exercises, strive to systematize and perfect the modes of discipline and teaching in the public schools.

11.—Decisions of the High Court of Justice in regard to Teachers.

(1.) *Signing an agreement with a Teacher is a mere approval of the appointment.*—The Court of Queen's Bench has decided that an inspector signing, together with trustee, a contract with a teacher, will be considered as having signed the same only as approving of the appointment, and not as contracting with the teacher.—*Campbell* v. *Elliott et al, County Model School, Middlesex.* 3 Q. B. R. 167.

(2.) *Trustees agreeing to furnish a Teacher with Fuel must be applied to for it.*—The Court of Queen's Bench has decided that when a teacher charged the trustees upon a special agreement stated to have been made by them, to furnish the said teacher with fuel when required, they could not be charged with a breach of covenant, as a request, with time and place, had not been stated in the teacher's declaration.—*Anderson* v. *Vansittart et al.* 5 Q. B. R. 335. Quære by the Court, whether such an agreement could be enforced?

(3.) *Trustee cannot be sued for Money due.*—The Court of Queen's Bench has decided that trustees refusing to give an order to a teacher for the school fund, according to their agreement with him, cannot be sued for money due, but for the refusal to give the order. *Quin* v. *Trustees, 4, Seymour.* 7 Q. B. R. 130.

(4.). *No rate can be imposed for the payment of an Unqualified Teacher.*—The Court of Queen's Bench has decided that no rate can legally be imposed by trustees for the salary of an unqualified teacher. *Chief Superintendent of Education, appellant, in re Stark* v. *Montague et al.* 14 Q. B. R. 473.

(5.) *Trustee and Teacher are not Master and Servant.*—The Court of Queen's Bench has decided that the Master and Servant Act (10 and 11 Vic., c. 23,) does not apply to school trustees and school teachers. Where a school trustee, therefore, has been convicted under it as a master, the conviction was quashed.—*In re Laurence Joice, No.—, Pittsburg, convicted by Robert Anglin, J. P.* 19 Q. B. R. 197.

(6.) *Representation as to the character of a Teacher by a Ratepayer is a Privileged Communication.*—The Court of Queen's Bench has decided that a representation by the assessed inhabitants of a school section as to the character of a teacher, made with a view of obtaining redress, is a privileged communication, which it is of importance to the public to protect; and such a statement would not be the less privileged if made by mistake to the wrong quarter. Where the libel complained of is clearly a privileged communication, the inference of malice cannot be raised upon the face of the libel itself, as in other cases it might be, but the plaintiff must give intrinsic evidence of actual express malice; he must also prove the statement to be false as well as malicious; and the defendant may still make out a good defence by proving that he had good ground to believe the statement true, and acted honestly under that persuasion. *Quære* by the Court, whether a communication of this nature, made by an inhabitant of any other part of the Province, would not be privileged.—*McIntyre v. McBean et al.* 13. Q. B. R. 534.

(7.) *Mandamus for Rate for Salary.*—The Court of Common Pleas has decided the following case: "The court refused a rule *nisi* for a *mandamus* to the trustees to levy a rate to pay the applicant the balance of his salary as teacher, recovered in the Division Court against former trustees, it not appearing when, for how long, and by whom the said teacher was employed."—*O'Donohoe v. School Trustees of Section No. 4, Thorah.* 5 C. P. 297.

(8.) *Enforcement of Agreements.*—The Court of Queen's Bench has decided the following case: "A school teacher sued the trustees in the Division Court for his salary, upon an agreement, under defendants' corporate seal, by which they bound themselves to employ the powers legally vested in them to collect and pay him; and upon the common count of work and labour. It appeared that he was not a legally qualified teacher, but that he had taught the school during the time claimed for. *Held*, that he could not recover: 1. Because by C. S. U. C. c. 64, s. 27, sub-sec. 9, as amended by 34 Vic. c. 33, s. 30, defendants were prohibited from giving an order in his favour on the local superintendent; and the latter, by sec. 91, sub-sec. 3, from giving him a check upon the treasurer. 2. Because, if entitled to payment, his remedy would be by *mandamus*, or a special action, not by an action for money, which was not in the defendants' hands. See also as to this point. *Quinn v. School Trustees*, 7 Q. B. 130. *Quære*, as to the meaning of 34 Vic. c. 33 s. 27, O."—*Wright v. The Trustees of School Section No. 3, in the Township of Stephen*, 32 Q. B. 541.

(9.) *Proceedings to Recover Salaries of Teachers.*—Declaration by a teacher against defendant, as sub-treasurer of school moneys, setting out an order signed by the local superintendent of schools in favour of plaintiff upon defendant, as such sub-treasurer, directing him to pay plaintiff $27 80, and charge to account of county assessment for 1866, and alleging a refusal to pay such order, with a claim for a mandamus. *Held*, declaration bad, as not shewing that the check or order was drawn on the order of the school trustees, and in setting out a check void on its face, because drawn upon a fund over which the local superintendent had no control, and in not shewing that defendant had money in his hands belonging to the school section, or that the county council had made provision to enable him to pay the amount.—*Welsh v. Leahey*, 18 C. P. 48.

Where an action in the Division Court by a teacher against the trustees was referred by order of the judge, with consent of the parties—*Held*, that the award could not be appealed from under 16 Vict., c. 153, s. 24. Remarks as to defendant's remedy by prohibition.—*The Chief Superintendent of Schools In re Milne and Sylvester*, 15 Q. B. 538.

Held, on demurrer to the avowry and cognizance set out in the report, that there is no right to arbitrate under C. S. U. C., c. 64, unless the contract of service is entered into by the trustees in their corporate capacity, made under their corporate seal; and without this the person discharging the duties of teacher has no legal status as such.—*Birmingham* v. *Hungerford et al.*, 19 C. P. 411.

(10.) *Contracts with Trustees.*—In an action by a school teacher to recover damages as for a wrong dismissal, it was shown that the agreement to employ the plaintiff was made in writing, under seal and signed by two, of the three school trustees, but not at the same time or at any meeting of the trustees called for the purpose of transacting school business :—*Held*, reversing the judgment of the County Court (Haldimand), that the agreement was void under sec. 97 of the Public Schools Act, which provides that " No act or proceeding of a school corporation which is not adopted at a regular or special meeting of the trustees, shall be valid or binding on any party affected thereby." *Lambiere* v. *The School Trustees of section No. Three, South Cayuga*, 7 A. R. 506. (See *School Trustees of the Township of Hamilton* v. *Neil*, 28 Chy., 408, p. 661.)

12.—Miscellaneous Duties of the Public School Teacher.*

(1.) *To hold Public Examinations.*—The teacher is required by law " to hold during each term a public examination of his school, of which he shall give due notice to the trustees of the school, to any school visitors who reside adjacent to the school, and through the pupils to their parents and guardians."† (Sch. Act, sec. 154, cl. [8].)

(2.) To give the trustees and visitors access at all times, when desired by them, to the registers and visitors' book appertaining to the school.—(*Ibid.* cl. [5].)

(3.) To deliver up any school registers, visitors' books, or school-house key, or other school property in his possession, on the demand or order of the majority of the trustee corporation employing him. (*Ibid.* cl. [6].)

NOTE.—" In case of his wilfully refusing to do so, he shall be deemed guilty of a misdemeanor, and shall not be deemed a qualified teacher until restitution be made, and shall also forfeit any claim which he may have against the said trustees." (*Ibid.* cl. [7].)

---

* As to the control of the teacher over the school-house, see decision No. 6, section 13, chapter ii., of the Court of Queen's Bench, on page 20.

† It will be seen by this clause of the Act that " it shall ['shall' here is imperative] be the duty of every teacher of a school : (8) 'To hold during *each term* a public examination of his school.' Teachers cannot, therefore, lawfully omit this part of their duty.

Form of Teacher's Circular Notice of the Quarterly Examination of his School.

School House of Section No. —

——————————, 18 .

SIR,—As required by law, the quarterly examinations of my school will be held on ———— day, th: — of ————, when the pupils of the school will be publicly examined in the several subjects which they have been taught during the quarter now closing. The exercises will commence at o o'clock a.m., and you are respectfully requested to attend them.

I am, Sir, your obedient servant,

A. B., *Teacher*.

To C. D., School Trustee, (or Visitor).

REMARKS.—A copy of the above notice ought to be sent to each of the trustees, and to as many visitors of the school as possible. The teacher should address a circular notice to those of them who reside within three miles of his school. He is also required to give notice, through his pupils, to their parents and guardians and to the neighbourhood, of the examination.

(4.) To furnish Information to the Minister, or Inspector.—"To furnish to the Minister of Education, or to the School Inspector, in the trustees' report or otherwise, any information which it may be in his power to give, respecting anything connected with the operations of his school, or in anywise affecting its interests or character." (*Ibid.* cl. [9].)

NOTE.—This duty involves the preparation of reports and returns, as provided in clause (6), section 9 of this chapter, p. 62, and section 21 of chapter ii., p. 23.

13.—Claim of Teacher for Salary until he is paid.*

"Every teacher shall be entitled to be paid at the rate mentioned in his agreement with the trustees (see section 4 of this chapter), even after the expiration of the period of his agreement, until the trustees pay him the whole of his salary, as teacher of the school, according to their engagement with him;" and including allowance for holidays and vacations, if provided for in the agreement with the trustees. (School Act, sec. 159.)

NOTE.—This section shall only apply where the teacher prosecutes his claim for salary within three months after it is due and payable by the trustees. (*Ibid.*)

14.—Teacher entitled to be paid for teaching days.

"Every qualified teacher of a public school employed for a period not less than three months, shall be entitled to be paid his salary in the proportion which the number of teaching days, during which he has taught, bears to the whole number of teaching days in the year." (*Ibid.* sec. 155.)

"In case of sickness, certified by a medical man, every teacher shall be entitled to his salary during such sickness, for a period not exceeding four weeks for the entire year; which period may be increased at the pleasure of the trustees." (*Ibid.* sec. 158.)

15.—Matters of difference in regard to Salary.

"All matters of difference between trustees and teachers, in regard to salary or other remuneration, shall be brought and decided in the division court by the judge of the county court in each county, subject to an appeal as provided by this Act." (*Ibid.* sec. 156.)

NOTE.—By section 4 of this chapter, it will be seen that no agreement between trustees and teachers, is lawful or binding on the school corporation, unless it is in writing and sealed with the trustees' corporate seal. None other can, therefore, be enforced in a court of law against the corporation. (See decisions of the superior courts, in section 11 of this chapter; see section 13, also.)

16.—Failure to carry out agreement with Trustees.

"Any teacher who enters into an agreement at common law with a board of trustees, and who wilfully neglects or refuses to carry out

---

* The Assessment Law does not exempt a school teacher either from the payment of a tax upon his salary (if over $400 per annum), or from the performance of two days of statute labour, if his salary be under $400.

such agreement, shall, on the complaint of any board of school trustees, be liable to the suspension of his certificate by the inspector in whose jurisdiction he may be engaged for the time being." (*Ibid.* sec. 166.)

NOTE.—Minister Crooks decided that "a school teacher possessing a Provincial certificate is in the same position as any other contracting party, and is liable to be sued in damages for refusing to fulfil an agreement. The question whether there is a contract or not would depend upon written evidence, signed by the teacher, or sent by original telegraph over his signature. Letters and telegrams will answer if sufficiently unequivocal. The proceedings against a teacher in case of failure to fulfil his engagement could be had in a division or a county court, or in one of the superior courts, according to the amount of actual damages which had resulted from such failure.*

CHAPTER X.
SUPERANNUATION OF TEACHERS AND INSPECTORS.

The School Act of 1885 contains the following provisions in regard to the superannuation of teachers and inspectors :—

192. From and after the date of this Act, every teacher or inspector whose name is entered as having paid into the fund for the support of superannuated teachers, may contribute to such fund in such manner as may be prescribed by the Education Department, the sum of at least four dollars annually.

193. On the decease of any teacher or inspector, his wife, her husband, or other legal representative, shall be entitled to receive back the full amount paid into the superannuation fund by such teacher or inspector, with interest at the rate of seven per cent. per annum.

194. Every teacher or inspector who, while engaged in his profession, contributes to the superannuated teachers' fund as provided by this Act, shall, on reaching the age of sixty years, be entitled to retire from the profession at his discretion, and receive an allowance or pension at the rate of six dollars per annum, for every year of such service in Ontario, upon furnishing to the Education Department satisfactory evidence of good moral character, of his age, and of the length of his service as teacher or inspector.

(2.) Every pension payable under this Act may be supplemented out of local funds by any municipal council, public school board or board of education, at its pleasure.

(3.) To remove doubts, nothing in this section contained shall be held as applying to any person, who, prior to 1871, had ceased to be engaged in his profession as a teacher, and has not heretofore con-

---

* Any questions as to legal liability on either side would be removed, if the form of Teachers' Contract-Agreement, prepared by the Author of this work, and published by Messrs. Copp, Clark & Co., Toronto, is used. It can be obtained from any bookseller.

tributed to the said fund; and no payment for arrears shall be received after the first day of July, 1886.

195. Every teacher or inspector under sixty years of age who has contributed as aforesaid, and who is disabled from practising his profession, shall be entitled to a like pension, or local supplementary allowance, upon furnishing the like evidence, and upon furnishing to the Education Department from time to time, in addition thereto, satisfactory evidence of his being disabled.

196. Every teacher entitled to receive an allowance from the superannuated teachers' fund, who holds a first or second-class provincial certificate, or a first-class county board certificate, or who is an authorized head master of a high school or collegiate institute, shall, in addition to said allowance or pension, be entitled to receive a further allowance at the rate of one dollar per annum for every year of service while he held such certificate, or while he acted as head master of a high school or collegiate institute.

197. The retiring allowance shall cease at the close of the year of the death of the recipient, and may be discontinued at any time should the pensioned teacher fail to maintain a good moral character, to be vouched for (when requested) to the satisfaction of the Education Department.

198. If any pensioned teacher or inspector shall, with the consent of the Education Department, resume the profession of teaching or inspecting, the payment of his allowance shall be suspended from the time of his being so engaged.

199. In case of his again being placed by the Education Department on the superannuation list, a pension for the additional time of teaching shall be allowed him, on his compliance with this Act, and the regulations of the Education Department.

200. Any teacher or inspector who, having resumed his profession, draws or continues to draw upon the superannuation fund for any part of his allowance as a superannuated teacher [or inspector], shall forfeit all claim to the fund, and his name shall be struck off the list of superannuated teachers [or inspectors].

201. In the case of those teachers or inspectors who may not avail themselves of the provisions of section 198 or 207 of this Act, the provisions of sections 198 to 207 inclusive shall apply, so far as relates to all sums of money already paid into the fund for the support of superannuated teachers.

202. Any teacher who retires from the profession, or any teacher, or inspector, who desires to remove his name from the list of contributors to the superannuated teachers' fund, shall be entitled to receive back from the Minister of Education one-half of any sums paid in by him or her to the fund, through the public school inspector, or otherwise.

CHAPTER XI.
RELATION OF INSPECTORS TO PUBLIC SCHOOL TEACHERS.

[NOTE.—No public school inspector shall, during his incumbency, hold the office of trustee of a high or public school, nor act as head master of a high school, or master or teacher of a public school. (Sch. Act, secs. 180 and 251.)

1.—Oversight of Public Schools by an Inspector.

The School Law requires each inspector of public schools "to see that every school is conducted according to law and the regulations of the Department. (See. 184, cl. [1].)

2.—Inspector's Visitation of Schools.

The law requires every county inspector "to visit every public school within his jurisdiction once in each term, unless oftener required to do so by the county council which appointed him, or for the adjustment of disputes, or other purpose." (*Ibid*, sec. 184, cl. [1].)

NOTE.—The regulations require the inspector to devote, on an average, half a day to the examination of the classes and pupils in each school, and to record the result of such examination in a book to be kept for that purpose. He shall also make inquiry and examination, in such manner as he shall think proper, into all matters affecting the condition and the operations of the school ; (but he shall not give any previous notice to the teacher or trustees of his visit.) (See Regulations.)

3.—Authority of an Inspector in a School.

The authority of an inspector in a school, while visiting it, is supreme ; the master, teachers, and pupils are subject to his direction ; and he shall examine the classes and pupils, and direct the masters or teachers to examine them, or to proceed with the usual exercises of the school, as he may think proper, in order that he may judge of the mode of teaching, management, and discipline in the school, as well as of the progress and attainments of the pupils.

4.—Inspector's Procedure in the Visitation of Schools.

On entering a school, with a view to its inspection, and having courteously introduced himself to the teacher (if a stranger), or, if otherwise, having suitably addressed him, the inspector shall :

(1.) Note in the inspector's book the time of his entrance, and on leaving, the time of departure from the school.

(3.) Examine the general and daily registers, and other school records, and take notes of the attendance of pupils, number of classes in the school at the time of his visit, &c.

(4.) Observe the mode of teaching, the management of the school, and generally its tone and spirit: also whether the bearing, manner, and language of the teacher, his command over the pupils, and their deportment at the time of his visit are satisfactory.

5.—Intercourse with Teachers and Pupils.

In his intercourse with masters and teachers, and during his visit to their schools, the inspector should treat them with kindness and respect, counselling them privately on whatever he may deem defective or faulty in their manner and teaching; but by no means should he address them authoritatively, or in a fault-finding spirit, in presence or hearing of the pupils.

6.—See to Attendance of Children at School.

The inspector should see that the provisions of the School Act, in regard to the rights of every child in the municipality under his jurisdiction, to attend some school, are not allowed to remain a dead letter.

NOTE.—The law requires each township clerk to furnish to the county inspector a statement, annually, of the number of children between the ages of 7 and 13 resident in each school section, and also a statement of the assessed value of the property in each school section, and also of the requisition on the council of the trustee board. (School Act, secs. 115 and 117.)

7.—Teachers Visiting other Schools.

County and city inspectors shall have authority to allow teachers to visit schools, under the restrictions contained in clause (2), section 10 of chapter ix., page 62.

8.—Cheques to Teachers payable to Themselves.

Any cheques for school money due a section must be made payable to the (qualified) teacher, assistant, or monitor, or his order, and to no other person; and no cheque shall be given to such teacher except on an order signed by a majority of the trustees of the school section, and attested by a lawful corporate seal, and then only for the time during which the teacher has held a legal certificate of qualification, not cancelled, suspended, recalled, or expired. (See note to sec. 22, of chapter ii., page 23.)

NOTE.—A form of order, which the trustees should send to the inspector, will be furnished by Messrs. Copp, Clark & Co., Toronto, free of postage, for 5 cents. (See note to section 22 of chapter ii., page 23.)

9.—Granting Special Certificates.

The School Law authorizes every inspector "to give, at his discretion, any candidate, on due examination, according to the programme authorized for the due examination of teachers, and subject to the regulations of the Education Department, a certificate of qualification to teach school within the limits of the charge of such inspector, until (but no longer than) the next regular meeting of the board of examiners of which such inspector is a member." (School Act, sec. 184, cl. 10.)

10.—Suspension of Public School Teachers' Certificates.

"The inspector of public schools may suspend the certificate of any teacher under his jurisdiction for inefficiency, misconduct, or a violation of the regulations of the Education Department, or of this Act. In every case of suspension he shall notify in writing the trustees concerned, and the teacher, of the reasons for such suspension." (*Ibid.* sec. 165.)

NOTE.—Officers, required by law to exercise their judgments, are not answerable for mistakes in law, or mere errors of judgment, without any fraud or malice.

11.—Inspector to Verify Attendance of Pupils.

The inspector should see that the aggregate attendance of each school is correctly added up, and divided by the divisor for the half year, and that no lost time is made up by teaching on Saturdays, or other holidays, or vacations. (See chapter xiv.) Under clause (2) of section 11 of chapter ix., teachers may, with the consent of the inspector, employ certain days in the year in visiting other schools. In order that the school may not lose a corresponding proportion of the school fund, the inspector is authorized to add a proportionate amount of average attendance for time so employed, or use a smaller divisor.

NOTE.—After having examined and tested the correctness of the return, the inspector should file away and carefully preserve it, so that it may be handed over, with other school documents, to his successor, when he retires from office.

12.—Check against Incorrect Returns.

The half-yearly return of the pupils' names, and number of days in which they attended during each month, will be a check against false or exaggerated returns; as the inspector can, in his visit to any school, take the return with him, compare it with the school register, and make any further inquiries he may deem necessary. He should, also, at his visits to the school, take notes in his book of the school attendance, &c.

NOTE.—The returns, carefully compiled, will furnish materials for the statistical tables in the inspector's report, and will show at what periods of the year the attendance of pupils at the schools is the largest, and how many attend school during two, four, six, &c., months of the year,

CHAPTER XII.
SCHOOLS IN UNORGANIZED TOWNSHIPS.

1.—Formation of School Sections in Unorganized Townships.

"In unorganized townships in any county or district it shall be lawful for the stipendiary magistrate thereof and the public school inspector (if any) of the county or district, or for the stipendiary magistrate alone if there be no inspector, and for the inspector alone if there be no stipendiary magistrate, to form a portion of a township, or of two or more adjoining townships, into a school section."

(*a*) No such section shall, in length or breadth, exceed five miles in a straight line.

(*b*) Subject to this restriction, the boundaries may be altered by the same authority from time to time, and the alteration shall go into operation on the twenty-fifth day of December next after such alteration.

(*c*) No such school section shall be formed except on the petition of heads of families resident therein. (School Act, sec. 41.)

2.—Election of Trustees in Unorganized Townships.

After the formation of such a school section, it shall be lawful for any two of the petitioners, by notice posted for at least six days in not less than three of the most public places in the section, to appoint a time and place for a meeting for the election, as provided by law, of three school trustees for the section. (*Ibid.* sec. 43.)

NOTE.—The elections of trustees under this section are to be conducted as pointed out in chapter vi., page 38.

3.—Powers of Trustees in Unorganized Townships.

The trustees elected at such meetings, or at any subsequent school meetings of the section, as provided by law, shall have all the powers and be subject to all the obligations of public school trustees generally. (*Ibid.* sec. 44.)

NOTE.—The powers and duties of trustees are fully explained in chapter ii.

4.—School Assessment Roll in Unorganized Townships.

The trustees so elected shall annually appoint a duly qualified person to make out an assessment roll for the section, and shall transmit a certified copy thereof to the stipendiary magistrate (or inspector).

(*a*) It shall be the duty of the stipendiary magistrate, or of the inspector, if there be no stipendiary magistrate, to examine the said roll, and correct any errors or improper entries which he shall perceive therein. (*Ibid.* sec. 45.)

NOTE.—For explanation in regard to collectors, etc., see chapter iii.

5.—Revision of the School Assessment Roll.

A copy of the said roll, as so corrected, shall be open to inspection by all persons interested, at some convenient place in the section, notice whereof, signed by the stipendiary magistrate, or inspector, if there be no stipendiary magistrate, is to be annually posted in at least three of the most public places in the section, and shall state the place and the time at which the magistrate or inspector will hear appeals against said assessment roll.

(*a*) Such notice shall be posted as aforesaid by the trustees for at least three weeks prior to the time appointed for hearing the appeals. (*Ibid.* sec. 46.)

6.—School Assessment Roll Appeals.

All appeals are to be made in the same manner and after the same notice, as nearly as may be, as appeals are made to a court of revision in the case of ordinary municipal assessments, and the magistrate (or inspector) shall have the same powers as such court of revision. (*Ibid.* sec. 47.)

7.—Power of Magistrate or Inspector in Appeal Cases.

(1.) The magistrate or inspector has power "to try all complaints in regard to persons wrongfully placed upon or omitted from the roll, or assessed at too high or too low a sum." (Assess. Act, R. S. O. ch. 180, sec. 53.)

(2.) *Oaths to Parties.*—The magistrate, or inspector, may, at his discretion, administer an oath to any party or witness before taking his evidence. The oath may, however, be required by the opposite party. (*Ibid*, secs. 54 and 56, cl. 16.)

(3.) *Summoning Witnesses.*—The magistrate, or inspector, may issue a summons to any witness, to attend at the confirmation of the roll, but if he fails to attend (having been tendered compensation for his time at the rate of fifty cents a day), he shall incur a penalty of $20, to be recoverable with costs by and to the use of any person suing for the same. (*Ibid.* secs. 54 and 55.)

NOTE.—This penalty can be recovered in the division court, or in any way in which penalties under municipal by-laws can be recovered. (*Ibid.*)

(4.) *Assessment on Real Property.*—In regard to real property, the magistrate, or inspector, "after hearing upon oath the complainant," and the party who assessed the property, "and any witness adduced, and, if deemed desirable, the party complained against, shall determine the matter, and confirm or amend the roll accordingly." (*Ibid.* sec. 56, cl. 15.)

(5.) *Assessment on Personal Property.*—If the party assessed complains of an overcharge on his personal property, or taxable income, he, or his agent, may make a declaration of the true value of personal property, without deducting ordinary debts (though debts on the property itself are to be stated), and of gross income from all sources; and no abatement shall be made from the amount of income in respect to debts, except debts due for or on account of such personal property; and the magistrate or inspector, shall, thereupon, enter the person assessed at such an amount of personal property, or taxable income, as is specified in such declaration, unless he shall be dissatisfied with the declaration; in which case the parties concerned, may be examined on oath as to "the correctness of the declaration," and the magistrate, or inspector, "shall confirm, alter or amend the roll, as the evidence shall seem to warrant." (*Ibid.* sec. 56, cl. 14.)

(6.) *Failure of Parties to Appear.*—"If either party fails to appear, either in person, or by an agent, the magistrate, or inspector, may proceed *ex parte*." (*Ibid.* sec. 56, cl. 17.)

8.—Confirmed School Assessment Roll Binding.

The annual roll, as finally passed and signed by the magistrate (or inspector), shall be binding upon the trustees and ratepayers of the section until the annual roll for the succeeding year is passed and signed, as aforesaid. (Sch. Act. sec. 48.

NOTE.—Where any township under the jurisdiction of a Township Board is unorganized, appeals against its certified assessment roll, made out by a person appointed by the Board, shall be made to the stipendiary magistrate or judge of the district or county, who has jurisdiction in other matters therein.

9.—Powers of Trustees in Unorganized Townships.

NOTE.—In addition to the powers possessed by rural school trustees and their duties, as set forth in chapters i. and ii , pages 5–23, those in unorganized townships have the following in addition :—

The trustees shall appoint some fit and proper person, or one of themselves, to be a collector (who may also be secretary-treasurer), to collect the rates imposed by them upon the ratepayers of their school section, or the sums which the inhabitants or others may have subscribed, or a rate-bill imposed on any person; and pay to such collector at the rate of not less than five or more than ten per centum on the moneys collected by him ; and every such collector shall give such security as shall be satisfactory to the trustees, which security shall be lodged for safe keeping with the stipendiary magistrate or the inspector by the trustees. (*Ibid.* sec. 51.)

10.—Powers of School Collectors.

Every such collector shall have the same powers in collecting the school rate. rate-bill, or subscriptions, shall be under the same liabilities and obligations, and shall proceed in the same manner in his school section and township as a township collector does in his municipality in collecting rates in a township or county, as provided in the Municipal Institutions and Assessment Acts from time to time in force. (*Ibid.* sec. 52.)

NOTE.—These "powers" are summarized as follows :—

(1.) Under a warrant from the trustees, the collector is authorised and required to collect the school rates imposed by them, or the sums which the inhabitants or others may have subscribed, and also the school rate bill payable by non-residents. The trustees are authorized to pay the collector at the rate of not less than *five* nor more than *ten* per cent. on the moneys collected by him.

(2.) The law gives the collector the same powers (by virtue of a warrant signed by a majority of the trustees) as a township collector, in collecting the school rate, rate bill, or subscription ; and it places him under the same liability and obligations.

(3.) The collector must proceed in the same manner in his school section and township, as a township collector does in collecting rates in a township or county, as provided in the Municipal Institutions and Assessment Acts from time to time in force. (School Act, sec. 52.)

(4.) The collector is required to give such security as may be satisfactory to the trustees, which security shall be lodged with the township council.

NOTE.—The Collector is entitled to his fee on all school rates entered on the roll when handed to him by the trustees, even should any of the rates be paid into the trustees, the secretary or teacher in the meantime. He must be careful to proceed in strict accordance with the law in the performance of his duty.

11.—Certificates to Teachers in New Districts.

Any public school inspector may, under such general regulations or instructions as may be prescribed according to law, examine and give special certificates, from time to time, to teachers in new and remote townships in the county, riding or division in which he is inspector ; which certificates shall be valid in such townships for the periods mentioned in the regulations. (*Ibid.* sec. 194, cl. 24.)

12.—Legal Decisions regarding School Rates and Collectors.

(1.) *Collector's Sureties not Responsible for Uncollected rates, nor for Collector's default, unless they so bind themselves in the bond.*—The Court of Common Pleas has decided the following case :—A person having been duly appointed collector by the trustees of a school section, signed the following contract at the foot of the instrument appointing him : "I agree, &c., &c., to *collect*, &c , according to the said Act, and bind myself, by my securities, in the sum of £250 ;" and immediately under his securities signed the following undertaking : " We hereby agree to become security for the due fulfilment of the above contract." The collector paid over a portion of the amount collected by him, leaving a certain sum remaining uncollected. An action was brought by the trustees against the collector and his sureties. *Held,* that the sureties, under their contract, were not jointly liable with their principal for moneys *uncollected* by him ; also, that they were not jointly liable on their guarantee as sureties on default of the principal— the contract only extending to the collection of the rate.—*Trustees No. 6, York v. William Hunter et al.* 10 C. P. R. 359.

(2.) *Note of Hand no legal Payment of School Rate.*—The Court of Queen's Bench has decided the following case on a *replevin* [see Index] for horses : *Plea,*— justifying the taking under a warrant for school taxes, and alleging that they were delivered by the collector to defendant, an innkeeper, to take care of until the sale. *Replication,*—setting out facts to show the rate illegal, and averring that plaintiff, after seizure of the goods, at the request of collector and trustees, gave his note for a sum named, (not saying that it was the amount due by him,) payable to bearer, which was accepted in satisfaction of the taxes ; that the collector released the property seized, and said note is still outstanding, and the plaintiff liable upon it, and that the seizure in the plea mentioned was made afterwards. *Held,* on demurrer, replication bad ; for, 1st, The collector, acting under a warrant legal on the face of it, would not be liable to trespass or trover, and therefore not in this action, nor the defendant for taking the horses from him to keep ; and, 2nd, Even if the note had been for a sufficient amount to pay the rate, yet the improper acceptance of it by the trustees would not prevent them from afterwards distraining.—*Spry* v. *McKenzie.* 18 Q. B. R. 161.

(3.) *Extension of time for collecting School Rates.—Duration of Collector's authority.*—The Court of Queen's Bench has decided the following case : The time for leving a school tax in the city of Kingston, imposed by by-law in December, 1855, was extended by resolution of the city council, under 18 Vic. c. 21, s. 3, until the 1st of August, 1856; and again on the 22nd of December, 1856, to the 1st of March, 1857. *Held,* that the collector, who was the same person for both years, might distrain between the 1st of August and the 22nd of December, 1956, although no resolution extending the time was then in force—*McLean, J.,* dissenting.—*Newberry Stephens et al, City of Kingston.* 16 Q. B. R. 65.

NOTE.—As a doubt was expressed by one judge in this case as to the legality of the extension of time, it would be better for trustees to issue a new warrant and take a fresh bond whenever the period mentioned in the bond expires.

(4.) *Right to collect School Taxes after the expiration of the Year.*—The Court of Queen's Bench has decided, on an appeal by the Chief Superintendent of Education, that a collector of school taxes might, in 1861, collect by distress the taxes for 1859 and 1860, not having made his final return of such taxes as in arrear, and being still collector ; and *semble,* that in this case the plaintiff, who complained of the seizure, having led to it by his own conduct, the proceeding should have been withheld in the division court at all events.—*Chief Superintendent of Education, appellant, in re McLean* v. *Farrell.* 21 Q. B. R. 441.

(5.) *Collector committing Trespass is entitled to notice of Action.—Limit.*—The Court of Common Pleas has decided that a collector who committed a trespass while acting under a warrant issued by a competent authority, was entitled to notice of action, and that the action should be brought within six months.—*Spry* v. *Mumby, et al, No. 15, Rawdon.* 11 C. P. R. 285.

(6.) *School Trustees have power to levy Rate at any time.*—Under the Acts relating to public schools, trustees may *at any time* impose and levy a rate for school purposes ; they are not bound to wait until a copy of the revised assessment roll for the particular year has been transmitted to the clerk of the municipality, but may and can use the existing revised assessment roll.—*Chief Superintendent of Education, appellant, in re Hogg* v. *Rogers.* 15 C. P. R. 417.

(7.) *Expenses of the School must be defrayed by the authority of the Trustees, and not by the inhabitants themselves.*—The Court of Queen's Bench has decided that freeholders and householders of a school section cannot substitute a voluntary subscription among themselves, and a rate upon the parents and guardians of children alone, for the whole expenses of the school, instead of the provisions made by law ; and a resolution to have such private subscription, which the trustees neglected to collect, is therefore no answer to an avowry by the trustees for a rate levied by them in the usual way.—*McMillan* v. *Rankin et al, No. 14 Kingston.* 19 Q. B. R. 356.

(8.) *School Tax upon Parents and Guardians unlawful.*—The Court of Common Pleas has also decided a similar case : A general school meeting passed the following resolution: "That the expenses of the school section be paid by voluntary subscription, and the balance to be raised from a *tax to be levied upon the parents and guardians* of those sending children to school." The school trustees, after the failure of the voluntary subscription, levied a general rate, upon which this replevin arose—the plaintiff contending that he was not liable, as *not being a parent or guardian* of a child attending the school. *Held*, that the trustees had no authority to tax the parents or guardians of those sending children, or to alter or annul the resolutions; and that the *tenth* clause of the *twenty-seventh* section of the School Act authorized the levy as made.—*Craig* v. *Rankin et al, No. 14, Kingston.* 10 C. P. R. 186.

(9.) *Form of, and number of, Signatures to Trustees' Warrant.*—The Court of Queen's Bench has decided that the warrant may be signed by two trustees [with the knowledge of the third]. In making cognizance under this warrant, it is sufficient to state that the plaintiff was duly assessed, and that the collector was duly appointed. It is not necessary to state therein that the rate was decided upon at a meeting, as required by statute, or how the appointment of collector was made.—*Gillies* v. *Wood, No. 6, Pilkington.* 13 Q. B. R. 357.

(10) *No Rate can be imposed by Trustees for the reimbursement of costs in defending Illegal Acts.*—The Court of Queen's Bench has decided that trustees cannot impose a rate to reimburse themselves for costs incurred in defending unsuccessfully a suit brought against them for levying an unauthorized rate, or for travelling expenses incurred in order to consult with the superintendent; but a rate may be levied to reimburse school trustees for the costs of defending a *groundless* action brought against them.—*Chief Superintendent of Education, appellant, in re Stark* v. *Montague,* 14 Q. B. R. 473; and *Tiernan* v. *Municipality of Nepean,* 15 Q. B. R. 87.

(11.) *Mandamus against Clerk of a Township to permit Trustees to examine the Assessment Roll.*—The Court of Queen's Bench has decided that where, on an application for a mandamus, a demand and a refusal were sworn to, and defendant in answer denied the refusal, and alleged that he had always been willing to do what was required, the Court nevertheless granted the writ.—*In re Trustees of Union School Section, Nos. 15, Otonabee, 10, Douro, and 11, Asphodel* v. *Casement,* 17 Q. B. R. 275.

NOTE.—A *mandamus* is a command issuing in the name of the Sovereign from a superior court having jurisdiction, and 1 is directed to some person, corporation, or inferior court, within the jurisdiction of such superior court, requiring them to do some particular thing therein specified, which appertains to their office and duty, or to show cause why they have not done it. This writ was introduced to prevent disorders from a failure of justice; therefore it ought to be used upon all occasions where the law has established no specific remedy, and where, in justice and good government, there ought to be one.

(12.) *Testator's Estate liable for School Rate in the hands of Devisees and Executors.*—The Court of Common Pleas decided as follows:—An action of replevin may be brought upon a distress for school rates, and notice of action is not necessary, where several devisees and executors were rated for a school rate in respect to the property of their testators as "John Applegarth and brothers," which entry appeared to have been made at the instance of some of them; but two of them only had slept on the premises occasionally, although such was not their ordinary place of residence, and they had received the usual notice of assessment in the form without appealing, and the same two had paid taxes on an assessment on the township roll in their indivi.lual names. *Held*, by the Court:—1st, That the facts afforded sufficient evidence to show that the plaintiffs were "inhabitants" for the purposes of the rate; 2nd, That the parties were sufficiently named on the roll to render the rate lawful; 3rd, That a demand made by the collector on "John Applegarth," named on the roll, was sufficient to bind all the plaintiffs.—*Applegarth et al,* v. *Graham, No. 3, Flamborough East.* 7 C. P. R. 171. (See "Non-Residents," chapter iv.)

(13.) *Liability of Executors and Devisees.*—The Court of Queen's Bench has decided that where executors and devisees in trust of land were assessed as owners:

Held, that they were properly so assessed, and that their own goods might be seized for the taxes.—*Dennison* v. *Henry*. 17 Q. B. R. 276.

(14.) *Overrated Taxes paid cannot be recovered back.*—The Court of Queen's Bench has decided that, if a person overrated pay the overrate without remonstrance or compulsion, he cannot afterwards recover it back.—*Grantham* v. *City of Toronto*, 2 Q. B. R. 475.

(15.) *Other cases cited.*—The following cases amongst others also bear upon the question of local municipal rates: *Ridsdale* v. *Brush*, (Roman Catholic Separate School case,) 22 Q. B. R. 122; *Fraser* v. *Page*, (general powers, etc.,) 18 Q. B. R. 336; *Holcolm* v. *Shaw*, (who ought to pay the taxes?) 22 Q. B. R. 92; also *Squire* v. *Mooney*, 30 Q. B. R. 531; *Jarvis* v. *Cayley*, (error in sale,) 11 Q. B. R. 282; *Coleman* v. *Kerr*, (affirming (3) on page 34,) 27 Q. B. R. 5; *Secretary of War* v. *Toronto*, (lien on land,) 22 Q. B. R. 555; *McBride* v. *Gardham*, (affirming (3) above page 34,) 8 C. P. R. 296; *Anglin* v. *Minis*, (validity of one demand not affected by change of occupant,) 18 C. P. R. 170; *Berlin* v. *Grange*, (non-residents,) 5 C. P. R. 211.

CHAPTER XIII.

GENERAL PROVISIONS OF THE LAW & REGULATIONS APPLICABLE TO ALL SCHOOLS.

1.—All Public Schools shall be Free Schools.

All "public schools shall be free schools, and every person between the ages of 5 and 21 years shall have the right to attend some school." (Sch. Act, sec. 6.)

2.—Residents in one Section sending to another Section.

"Any person residing in one school section or division, and sending a child or children to the school of a neighbouring one, shall, nevertheless, be liable for the payment of all rates assessed on his taxable property for school purposes in the section or division in which he resides, as if he sent his child or children to the school of such section or division. (*Ibid.* sec. 125.)

NOTE.—Children from rural sections attending public schools in cities, towns or incorporated villages shall " be reported as attending the public school of the school section in which they are actual residents." (*Ibid.* sec 203, cl. 2.) See chapter iv., on "Non-residents," page 31.

3.—Exception as to Supporters of Separate Schools.

Nothing in this Act authorizing the levying or collecting of rates on taxable property for public school purposes shall apply to the supporters of Roman Catholic separate schools. (School Act, sec. 3.)

4.—Authorized Text Books to be used.

No teacher shall use or permit to be used as text books any books in a model or public school, except such as are authorized by the Education Department, and no portion of the legislative or municipal grant shall be paid by the inspector to any school in which unauthorized books are used. (*Ibid.* sec. 206.)

Any authorized text book in actual use in any public or model school may be changed by the teacher of such school for any other authorized text book in the same subject on the written approval of the trustees and the inspector, provided always such change is made at the beginning of a school term, and at least six months after such approval has been given. (*Ibid.* sec. 207.)

In case any teacher or other person shall negligently or wilfully substitute any unauthorized text book in place of any authorized text book in actual use upon the same subject in his school, he shall for each such offence, on conviction thereof before a police magistrate or justice of the peace, as the case may be, be liable to a penalty not exceeding ten dollars, payable to the municipality for public school purposes, together with costs, as the police magistrate or justice may think fit. (*Ibid.* sec. 208.)

5.—Religious Instructions in the Schools.

Pupils shall be allowed to receive such religious instructions as their parents and guardians desire, according to any general regulations provided for the organization, government and discipline of public schools. (*Ibid.* sec. 8.)

NOTE.—No person shall require any pupil in any public school to read or study in or from any religious book, or to join any exercise of devotion or religion objected to by his or her parents or guardians. (*Ibid.* sec. 7.)

6.—Opening and Closing Exercises of each day.

Every public and high school shall be opened with the Lord's Prayer, and closed with the reading of the Scriptures and the Lord's Prayer, or the prayer sanctioned by the Department of Education. (*Regulations approved by the Lieutenant-Governor in Council, 16th December, 1884.*)

NOTE.—A volume containing the Scripture readings and the prayers sanctioned by the Department has been provided by the Department. The trustees are required to place a copy of it in each department of their school.

7.—Weekly Instruction by the various Clergy.

The clergy of any persuasion, or their authorized representatives, shall have the right to give religious instruction to the pupils of their own church, in each school house, at least once a week, after the hour of closing the school in the afternoon ; and if the clergy of more than one denomination apply to give religious instruction in the same school house, the School Board Trustees shall decide on what day of the week the school house shall be at the disposal of the clergyman of each denomination at the time above stated. But it shall be lawful for the School Board or Trustees and clergyman of any denomination to agree upon an hour of the day at which a clergyman, or his authorized representative, may give religious instruction to the pupils of his own church, provided it be not during the regular hours of the school. *(Ibid.)*

NOTE.—The Regulations prescribing the " Hours of Daily Teaching " provide that they shall not exceed six hours in duration, but "a less number of hours of daily teaching may be determined upon in any Public School at the option of the Trustees " Arrangements may, therefore, be made by the Trustees for closing the ordinary school work earlier than the usual hour on certain days, so that time may be given for religious instrucrion.

8.—No School Official shall act as Book Agent.

" No teacher, trustee, inspector, or other person officially connected with the Education Department, the normal, model, public or high schools or collegiate institutes, shall become or act as agent for any person or persons to sell, or in any way to promote the sale for such person or persons of any school library, prize or text book, map, chart, school apparatus, furniture or stationery, or to receive compensation or other remuneration or equivalent for such sale, or for the promotion of sale in any way whatsoever." (Sch. Act, sec. 267.)

9.—When School Fund to Schools may be Withheld.

The Public School Inspector is required "To withhold his order for the amount apportioned from the Legislative or Municipal grant to any school section :—

"*(a)* When the school was kept open for less than six months in the year ;

"*(b)* When the trustees fail to transmit the annual or semi-annual school returns properly filled up ;

"*(c)* When the trustees fail to comply with the School Act, or the Regulations of the Education Department ;

"*(d)* When the teacher uses, or permits to be used, as a text book any book not authorized by the Education Department." *(Ibid.* sec. 184, cl. 4.)

10.—Penalty for Disturbing Public Schools.

" Any person who wilfully disturbs, interrupts, or disquiets the proceedings of any school meeting authorized to be held by this Act, or any one who interrupts or disquiets any public school established and conducted under its authority, by rude or indecent behaviour or by making a noise either within the place where such school is kept or held, so near thereto as to disturb the order or exercises of the school, shall, for each offence, on conviction thereof before a justice of the peace, on the oath of one credible witness, forfeit and pay for public school purposes to the school section, city, town or village within which the offence was committed, a sum not exceeding twenty dollars, together with the costs of conviction, as the said justice may think fit." (*Ibid.* sec. 250.)

CHAPTER XIV.

SCHOOL TERMS AND HOLIDAYS.

The public school year shall consist of two terms: the first shall begin on the third day of January, and end on the first Friday of July; the second shall begin on the third Monday of August, and end on the twenty-third day of December. Every Saturday, every statutory holiday, and every day proclaimed a holiday by the municipal authorities in which the school section or division is situated, shall be a holiday in the public schools. (School Act, sec. 205.)

NOTE.—In cities, towns and incorporated villages the school terms shall be the same as the terms prescribed for high schools. (*Ibid.*)

CHAPTER XV.

COUNTY MODEL SCHOOLS.

The [county] board of examiners shall, under the regulations of the Education Department and subject to the approval of the Minister of Education, set apart at least one school in each county as a county model school for the training of candidates for third class teachers' certificates, and the county council shall provide and levy in each year, in aid of each county model school within the limits of the county, an amount at least equal to the amount apportioned or paid by the Education Department, in support of county model schools out of any grant annually voted by the legislature for that purpose, but the amount to be provided by the county council shall not be less than the sum of one hundred and fifty dollars in one year, unless the county council should see fit to provide a larger amount of aid. (School Act, sec. 174.)

CHAPTER XVI.

TEACHERS' INSTITUTES.

It shall be lawful for the Minister of Education to apportion out of any moneys voted by the Legislative Assembly for the training of teachers the sum of twenty-five dollars for every teachers' institute established under the regulations of the Education Department, and it shall be the duty of the county or city council of each city or county to pay to the order of the president of each such institute within the county or city, a sum at least equal to the amount so apportioned by the Minister of Education. (School Act, sec. 175.)

CHAPTER XVII.

TEACHERS' ASSOCIATIONS.

The following are the Departmental Regulations :—

1. *Objects of Association.*—In each county or inspectoral division a Teachers' Association shall be formed, the object of which shall be to read papers and discuss matters having a practical bearing on the daily work of the school room.

2. *Officers.*—The officers of the Association shall be a president, vice-president, and secretary-treasurer. There shall also be a management committee of five. The officers of the Association and the management committee shall be elected annually.

3. *Meetings.*—There shall be at least one meeting of the Association each year, extending over two or more days, to be called the annual meeting, for the election of officers and the discussion of such matters as may be submitted by the management committee.

4. *Sessions.*—The session of the annual meeting on the first day shall be from 10 a. m. to 12 m., and from 2 p. m. to 5 p. m.; on the second day from 9 a. m. to 12 m., and from 2 p. m. to 4 p. m.

5. *Time and place.*—The time and place for holding this meeting, and the programme for the same, shall be arranged by the Education Department on consultation with the Inspector or Inspectors of the county or divisional Association. A copy of the programme should be sent to every teacher in the county or inspectoral division

at least one month before the time of meeting. The work of the Association shall be as practical as possible; and at every meeting illustrative teaching of classes should form a prominent part of the proceedings. All questions and discussions foreign to the teachers' work should be avoided.

6. *Township Meetings.*—Another meeting, arrangements for which should be made at the annual meeting of the Association, for the county or inspectoral division may be held during the year; or in lieu thereof a series of Township Associations may be held in the townships or union of townships in the county.

7. *Teachers to attend.*—It shall be the duty of every teacher to attend continuously all the meetings of the Association held in his county or inspectoral division (two days in each half year so spent to be counted as visiting days) and in the event of his inability to do so, to report to his Inspector, giving reasons for his absence.

8. *Inspector's duty.*—It shall be the duty of the Inspector to furnish the secretary of the Association with a list of the teachers in his county or inspectoral division. From this list the roll shall be called at the opening of each session. He shall also report to the Department on the form prescribed.

8. The following order of business is recommended. :—

First day.—1. Opening; 2. Appointment of committees; 3. Business; 4. Reading and discussion of papers; 5. Lecture in the evening by the Departmental Director of Teachers' Association.

Second day.—1. Opening; 2. Receiving reports of committees; 3. Business; 4. Reading and discussion of papers; 5. Election of officers; 6. Closing.

10. *Director.*—The Departmental Director of Teachers' Associations shall attend the annual meeting of each Association, and shall discuss at least three subjects on the programme, and deliver a public lecture on the evening of the first day.

ANALYTICAL INDEX.

	PAGE.
ABSENCE of trustee for three months without leave vacates office	7
of teacher	62, 66
of pupils	58
ABSENTEES. (See NON-RESIDENTS), requirement of school law as to children	54
trustees to compel attendance of children and report	55
power and duty of magistrates as to	55
ACCOMMODATION, adequate school, to be provided	16, 54
pupil not entitled to admission unless adequate	20
what constitutes adequate	17, 18
ACCOUNT, penalty for trustees refusal to	34
ACCOUNTABILITY for school moneys	34
ACTION, notice of, trustees entitled to	11, 15, 16
collector entitled to	16
ADJOURNMENT. (See SCHOOL MEETING.)	
AGE at which pupils can attend school	78
AGENT.	
trustees, teacher, inspector, &c., cannot act as booksellers	80
AGREEMENT:	
form of, between trustees and teacher	56
must be in writing (or printed) and under seal	56
signature of local superintendent a mere approval of the	63
AIR, cubic feet for each child	18
ALTERATION. (See TOWNSHIP COUNCIL BOUNDARIES, DEBTS.)	
of school section boundaries, decision of the Superior Courts in regard to	20
by-law for, bad if boundaries are not certainly defined	141
of boundaries no ground for refusal to levy rate	20
in award, effect of	51
ALTERED school section, who are trustees of	8
disposition of property in	17
AMENDMENTS to motions at school meetings	42
ANNUAL FINANCIAL ACCOUNT. (See SCHOOL TRUSTEES, &c.)	
REPORT of rural trustees and auditors to be read at annual meeting	40
by rural trustees to inspector	23
school meeting to be called	38
fixed for last Wednesday in January	38
order of business in rural school sections	40
rules to be observed in rural school sections	40, 41, 42

ANALYTICAL INDEX.

PAGE.

APPARATUS. (*See* TEXT BOOKS, LIBRARIES.)
    trustees to do what they think expedient in regard to............ 36
APPEAL, none to Minister 44
    to inspectors in school election complaints 43, 50
    to stipendiary magistrates or inspectors......................... 73
ARBITRATION. (*See* AWARD, ARBITRATORS.)
    between trustees and owner of school site 46
    between rural trustees and people in regard to site 50
    may be superseded before award be made 48, 51
    proceedings of first, on school site.............................. 51
    adjournment of 46
    summary of general rules in regard to.......................... 47
    costs of 48
    none unless contract under seal................................. 65
ARBITRATORS. (*See* AWARDS.)
    constitution of board of 47
    must meet to decide about school site, remedy 46
    remedy is case parties refuse to appoint 46
    remedy in case of the refusal to act 46
    who may be 47
    county inspector to be one of the 47
    duties and power of the 46, 47
    must hear evidence 47
    cannot delegate their power................................ 47, 48
    general rules in regard to................................. 47, 48
    making and publishing award... .... 47, 192
    have no power to alter award after making it.................... 51
    expenses of, who shall pay. (*See* AWARD.)................. 46, 48
    entitled to a *per diem* allowance.
    misconduct of... 48
    must meet for discussion....................................... 46
    decisions of Superior Courts in regard to....................... 51
ARREARS :
    of school taxes, how collected.................................. 76
    of non-resident tax, how collected.............................. 26
ASSESSED freeholders and householders 39
ASSESSMENT in unorganized township 74
    roll, trustees to have access to 77
ASSISTANTS in schools... 56
ASSOCIATIONS, regulations for teachers'........................... 82
ATTENDANCE OF PUPILS AT SCHOOL :
    trustees to report to inspector 23
    inspector to verify... 71
    teacher to keep register of 61
    inspector to apportion according to average 71
    compulsory at school...................................... 54, 55

ANALYTICAL INDEX.   87

	PAGE.
AUDIT, trustees to present yearly accounts for 33,	43
summary of the law in regard to School Section.................	35
AUDITORS' rural school report to be submitted to the annual meeting 33	43
contents of report..	43
by whom appointed	33
trustees to submit school accounts and give information to........	34
either of the, to call meeting for examining accounts	33
object of await	33
duty of..	33
powers of...	35
time of audit	33
remedy if trustees neglect to appoint one	33
penalties on trustees refusing information to	34
may summon witnesses take evidence on oath and enforce decisions	34
to remain in office until audit is completed.....................	33
inspector to decide differences between	43
AUTHORITY of inspector in schools	69
AVERAGE ATTENDANCE, the basis of distributing the school fund..	71
AWARD. (*See* Arbitration, Arbitrators.)	
of arbitrators in regard to site to be registered	17
when it can be set aside	48
making and publishing an 48, 189,	193
time and mode of making an .... :.............. 48,	51
when it is bad 48	51
before being made may be superseded by consent................	48
effect of mistake on alteration in	51
when it may be signed by two arbitrators 46,	47
may be re-considered by consent within three months......... ..	49
may be referred back when.....................................	49
appeal from...	64
cost of	48
power of school meetings as to........................ 49, 51,	52
BANKING, acts of by trustees, forbidden............................	15
BELL, school..	22
BOARD and lodging of teachers	56
BOOKS. (*See* Apparatus, Text-Books, Libraries.)	
pupils must be supplied with 21, 103, 203,	204
authorized text, to be used....................................	22
trustee, teacher, inspector, cannot act as agent for	80
BOUNDARIES.	
trustee placed outside by alteration in.........................	8
BUILDING. (*See* School House.)	
CALLING school meetings by trustees	38
CASTING VOTE. (*See* Vote.)	

ANALYTICAL INDEX.

	PAGE.
CERTIFICATES for different classes of teachers	70
temporary, may be granted by inspectors	70
CHAIRMAN and secretary to be appointed at rural school meeting	39
duties of, and right to vote	39
penalty on, for not sending copy of proceedings to inspector	41
trustees' declaration of office to be made before	7
(*See* SCHOOL MEETING SECRETARY.)	
CHEQUES to teachers papable to themselves	70
can only be given so a qualified teacher	70
CLEANING school house	19
CLERGYMEN are school visitors	79
entitled to give religious instruction to pupils	79
COLLECTOR, appointment and duties of school	26
protection of, in performance of duty	75
committing trespass is entitled to notice of action	76
has the same powers and liabilities as township collector	75
security, must give bond of	75
fees of	26, 74, 75
powers, duties, and liabilities of	76
duration of authority of	76
can be compelled to make return	75
securities of, when not responsible	75
number of signatures to warrant of	26, 75
form of warrant of	77
fees of, must be included in rate	30
COLOURED PEOPLE, right of admission to school	21
COMPLAINTS, to inspectors, to decide upon school election	43
cannot be entertained, unless within *twenty days* of school meeting	43
may be decided by inspector	43
COMPULSORY sale of school site	49
attendance of pupils at school	36
CONTESTED ELECTIONS. (*See* ELECTIONS.)	
CONTRACTS with teachers. (*See* AGREEMENT, SCHOOL MEETINGS, CORPORATE SEAL.)	
void unless made at meeting of trustees	65
by trustees, between themselves unlawful, except in certain cases	13
verbal	9, 10
enforcement of	64
CORPORATE POWERS, liability of trustees in case of neglect to exercise	11, 14
act, trustees, when sued for, entitled to notice. (*See* CORPORATIONS)	11, 15, 16
SEAL must be used by trustees in all official acts	36
renders contract binding	20
must be used in agreements between trustees and teacher	56

ANALYTICAL INDEX. 89

PAGE.

CORPORATION. (*See* SCHOOL TRUSTEES.)
    school trustees to be a, general power of 14
    definition of the term 16
    decision of the courts, in regard to school 15
    aggregate, cannot be subpœnaed, but its members can 15
    acts of banking by trustee, forbidden 14
    acts of the majority, binding upon the.......................... 9
    notice of trustee meetings must be given to all the members of 9
    bound by the affixing of the corporate seal..................... 20
    all common school property vested absolutely in school 16
COSTS, law, incurred by trustees.................................... 77
    of arbitration 48
COUNCIL, TOWNSHIP. (*See* MUNICIPAL COUNCIL.)
    obligation of 27
    board of school trustees to lay estimate before 27
    has no discretion in raising rums required by trustees........... 27
    mandamus against... 31
    MUNICIPAL may lend to school trustees 27, 28

DEBENTURES :
    to be issued by township council for trustees' loans 28, 29
DEBTS, liability of original section for old 8, 20
DECISIONS of Superior Courts on school questions.
    as to personal liability of trustees 9, 11
    regarding school trustee corporations 15
    regarding school house... 19
    regarding secretary-treasurer................................... 25
    regarding school rates 30, 75
    regarding school sites 51
    regarding teachers... 63
DECLARATION of voter at school election of meeting 39
    of office, by rural trustees only required...................... 7
    before whom to be made by rural trustee........................ 7
    effect when not made by trustee 7
DEED, absence of.. 17
    register award as substitute for................................ 17
DEFAULTING secretary-treasurer and collector...................... 25
DEVISEES, executors, liability of their testatory estate 77
DISCIPLINE to be maintained in the school by the teacher........... 58
DISPUTES. (*See* COMPLAINT.)
    inspector may settle school..................................... 43
DISPOSAL of school property provided for 17
DISTURBING A SCHOOL OR SCHOOL MEETING. penalty for...... 80
DIVIDING A SCHOOL SECTION. (*See* ALTERATION, TOWNSHIP COUNCIL.)
DIVISION COURT. litigation with teachers to be in 66

	PAGE
ELECTIONS, school, who shall call meetings for	38
time of keeping open the poll at	38
mode of trustee	43
of chairman and secretary at school meeting	39
complaint as to mode to inspector	43
notification of, to the county inspector	41
at an ordinary annual meeting	42
in unorganized townships	72
mode of proceeding in contested, in rural sections	43
no appeal from decision of inspector or contested	43
county inspector to decide upon complaints of	43
three trustees to be elected at first, and one afterwards	8
ELECTORS, school defined. (See SCHOOL MEETINGS)	39
EMBEZZLEMENT of moneys by trustees	12
ENLARGING. (See SITE.)	
ERECTION. (See HOUSE.)	
EVIDENCE, on oath before school section auditors	34
on oath before arbitrators	47
EXAMINATION, of pupils each term	65
of schools by inspectors	69
EXECUTORS, as well as testators, liable for rate on non-resident land	77
estate in hands of liable	77
EXERCISES in school, religious	79
EXPEDIENCY or lawfulness of trustees' expenditure	35
EXPULSION of pupils	59
EXPENSES, definition of school, in rural sections	22
trustees shall determine school	22
of school to be collected by trustees' authority	27
FALSE declaration of right to vote	39
FEES payable by non-residents 22, 27,	32
collector's 26, 74,	75
FELONY or misdemeanor, trustee convicted of, effect	7
FENCE round school premises	17
FINANCIAL REPORT. (See AUDITORS, ANNUAL REPORTS.)	
FINE, for refusal to serve as trustee	7
for neglect of duty by trustee	7
FIRST school meeting, notice in regard to	72
FORM of declaration required from school electors	39
of declaration of office of rural trustee	7
of bond of collector or secretary-treasurer	27
of debentures for trustees' loans	27
of deed for site of a school house, teachers' residence, &c.	17
of agreement between trustee and teacher 57,	67
of notice of annual meeting	38
of notice of quarterly examination	65
for taking school census	54

FORM—(Continued).
    of warrant for collection of school rate.............................. 77
    of estimate requisition to council............................ 27, 30
FREE SCHOOLS, establishment of, by statute 78
    free public school libraries 22
FUEL. (See WARMING.)
    providing, for school 19, 22
    trustees agreeing to furnish a teacher with, must be applied to for 63
    charge for, must be provided by rate 45
FURNISHING furniture for school house 21

GROUNDS, school house, to be kept in order 19

HALF-YEARLY REPORT to be made by trustees to inspector 23 36
    trustees personally responsible for not making 36
    VISIT of inspectors 69
HEATING school house. (See FUEL, WARMING.)
HOLIDAY'S AND VACATIONS :
    no deduction can be made from teacher's salary for legal.......... 66
    regulations in regard to 81
    every Saturday is a holiday..... 81
HOURS of opening and closing school meetings................... 38, 41
    of teaching 60
HOUSE, SCHOOL, kind of 17, 18
    form of deed for... 17
    second in a section 23, 28
    not liable to be sold under a judgment........................... 20
    care and repair of 19
    separate entrance to 18
    exempt from taxation 21
    contracts, for school, require seal 19
    submission to electors of section of proposals for 21
    trustees alone may build or rent 19
    trustees may levy rate to build 19
    not required, may be disposed of 49
    warming, sweeping and cleaning 19, 61
    trespass on, proper remedy for 20
    use of, for other than church purposes........................ 20
    renting, repairing, furnishing &c. 19
    township councils can levy rate for 28
    special expenditures for 29
    legal decisions, respecting 19
    limitations as to expenditures for 29
    FOR TEACHER'S RESIDENCE, provision for 19

ILLEGAL ACTS, of trustees, no rate can be imposed for defending 77
INDIVIDUAL responsibility of trustees. (See TRUSTEES.)

ANALYTICAL INDEX.

	PAGE.
INJURY to school property 60,	61
INSPECTOR, public school, cannot be a trustee or teacher 56,	69
duty and general powers of.................................	69
duty and authority of	69
copy of proceedings of all school meetings to be sent to	44
may call special school meeting	38
decide school electon complaints	43
no appeal from decision of, to Minister.......................	44
may consent to estabishment of a second or female school	23
trustees to give orders on	23
trustees to make half-yearly and yearly reports to	23
to appoint a school auditor in certain cases....................	33
may call meeting to select school site	46
to be or appoint arbitrator as to school site...................	46
to be remunerated for arbitration, &c	46
duty in forming school sections in unorganized townships	72
to furnish township clerk with certain information	90
to be furnished with information by master or teacher...........	66
not to hold certain offices 69,	80
not to act as agent for sale of books, &c.......................	80
to apportion, but not pay, unless trustees make average return....	80
to give cheques to qualified teachers only	70
when orders to be withheld by	80
to visit each school once in each term	69
not to give any notice of school visit..........................	69
to examine into state of school	69
authority of, in a school	69
procedure in visiting schools	69
intercouse with teachers and pupils	70
see to compulsory attendance of children at school	70
allow teachers to visit other schools..........................	70
payment to superanuated teachers' fund 67,	68
verify attendance of pupils..................................	71
check by, against incorrect returns	71
appeal from school section auditors	43
to see to observance of lawful regulations	71
to act according to law and regulations	69
to decide disputes 44,	69
may suspend teacher's certificate	71
to give temporary certicates to teachers	70
signing agreement with teacher	63
decide as to non-residents' liability	32
inspection of schools by 69, 70,	71
INSTITUTES, aid to	81

ANALYTICAL INDEX. 93

PAGE.
JUDGES, county, to decide in Division Court disputes between trustees
    and teachers 66
    application to, and hearing of complaint by, against secretary-
    treasurer 24, 25

LAND taken for school site 46
LAWFULNESS of school trustees' expenditure; auditors' duty........ 35
LEGAL decisions. (*See* DECISIONS.)
LIABILITY of school collectors 75
    of non-residents' property 26, 32
LIBRARIAN, rural trustees to appoint 22
    teacher to act as 61
LIBRARIES, trustees to establish in school section................... 22
    trustees may purchase books for 37
    fees for chargeable on non-residents..................... 22
LOAN by trustees to be authorized by township council 27, 28
    by council to trustees 27, 28
    authority to raise a rate to pay off 28
LORD'S PRAYER to be used in daily religious exercises............. 79
LOST moneys, trustees responsible for 34

MAJORITY of trustees, acts of the, binding on the school corporation.. 15
MAKING and publishing an award........................ 47, 48
MANDAMUS. (*See* WRIT OF MANDAMUS.)
MASTERS. (*See* SCHOOL TEACHERS.)
    and Servant Act does not apply to teachers 63
    and teacher, distinction between 57
MEETINGS. (*See* SCHOOL MEETINGS.)
MINISTER OF EDUCATION, no appeal to 44
MINUTES of proceedings, copy of, to be sent to inspector 41
MODEL school, board of examiners in county may establish 81
    established by county board of examiners 81
MONEY. (*See* SCHOOL FUND, SCHOOL MONEYS.)
    lost, trustees' responsibility for........................ 34
    may be lent by municipalities to trustees 27, 28
    MONITORS in schools 56
MOTIONS at school meetings should be seconded 42
    may be reconsidered or rescinded...................... 41
    order of putting.................................. 42
MUNICIPAL. (*See* TOWNSHIP COUNCIL.)
    accountability of treasurer for school moneys 30
    authorities may loan money to school trustees 27, 28
    mandamus to corporation 31

NEGLECT of duty by trustee 11, 14
    to make verbal declaration of office by rural trustee 7, 35, 42

ANALYTICAL INDEX.

	PAGE.
NEW SCHOOL SECTIONS, magistrate and inspector in unorganized townships	72
NON-ATTENDANCE of three months will cause vacation of trustees' office	7
NON-RESIDENCE, bar to acting as trustees	7
pupil defined	22, 31
NON-RESIDENTS. (*See* APPRENTICES, &C.)	
defined	31
collection of fees chargeable on	26
rights of	32
authority of trustees in regard to	32
how to proceed against	26
fees chargeable on	22, 27, 32
goods and chattles of, liable to seizure	26
liability of, if owning taxable property	32
legal decisions in regard to rates of	30, 75
uncollected rates of, return of	75
law relating to, does not apply to separate school supporters	32
lands of	32
trustees to collect rates of	26, 27
inspectors to decide as to distance from school	32
children of, to be returned as pupils in their own section	32
liable in their own section, but may send to any section taxing them	32
LAND, executors liable for school rate on	77
NOTES of hand not to be issued by trustees	10
of hand no payment of school rate	75
NOTICE. (*See* FORM.)	
of annual school meeting	38
of special school meeting	44
to inspector of the proceedings of school meeting	41
by two electors in case of neglect to call meeting	38
of trustee meetings to all members of the corporation	9
of action, individual, trustees and collectors entitled to (*See* CORPORATION)	11, 15, 16
of the school visits of inspector should not be given	69
OATH, school section auditors may require evidence on	34
OMISSIONS in tax roll, how remedied	73
ORCHARD. (*See* SITE.)	
ORDER, rules of, for school meetings	40, 41, 42
ORDERS for school fund by trustees	23, 36
PARENTS OR GUARDIANS, tax upon, unlawful	76
protection of, respecting religious instruction	79
PAROL, award. (*See* AWARD.)	

ANALYTICAL INDEX.

PENALTIES. (*See* RESPONSIBILITY.)
  ON TRUSTEES, for refusing to serve as trustee 7
    in case of neglect to exercise corporate powers............... 7, 10
    for neglecting to forward to inspector returns.................... 41
    for losing school moneys through neglect of duty................. 34
    for refusing information to auditors 34
    for signing a false report 11
    for non-observance of regulations 10
    on chairman for not sending to inspector copy of school meeting
      proceedings... 40
    for false declaration of right to vote at school meetings 39
    on secretary-treasurer, for refusing to account 24
    on teacher, for refusing to deliver up school property 65
    on any person for disturbing a school or school meeting.......... 80
PLAY GROUND required.. 45
POLICE MAGISTRATE and compulsory education 55
POLL hours at school election 38
POWERS OF TRUSTEES. (*See* SCHOOL TRUSTEES.)
PRESENTS, subscriptions, &c., to teachers forbidden 63
PROCEEDINGS of annual meeting. (*See* MEETING.)
PROMISSORY NOTES, trustees may not issue 10
  no payment of school rates..................................... 75
PROTECTION of trustees, collectors and magistrates.......... 11, 15, 16
PROTEST at school meetings 41
PUBLISHING, and making an award.............................. 47, 48
PUPILS. (*See* EXAMINATION, TEACHERS.)
  resident, between 5 and 21 to be admitted to school 17
  non-resident, where to be returned 31
  suspension of, by teacher 58
  expulsion of, by trustees.. 59
  to be classified 59
  not obliged to attend religious exercises 79
  trustees cannot be compelled to admit unless accommodation adequate 21

QUALIFIED TEACHERS only to be employed... 36
  trustees' orders to be given to, and to no others 23
  definition of the term 10

RATEPAYERS. (*See* SCHOOL MEETING.)
  consent of, not necessary for school rates 28
RATES, school and collector's, legal decisions respecting .... 75 *et seq.*
  trustees may levy at any time 76
  who are liable for 78
  for what, may be collected 29
  note of hand, no payment of 75
  collector shall call for 27

RATES—(*Continued*).
    on non-residents, how collected................................. 26
    on parents and guardians, except of non-resident children, unlawful 76
    cannot be levied to pay unqualified teacher 63
    unpaid, how obtained 74
    application to township council to collect 29, 30
    on supporters of separate schools 78
    cannot be levied to defend illegal action or excessive interest 78
    cannot be levied, trustees' claim (exception) 29
    requisite of warrant for 77
    trustees', mode of collecting 77
    extension of time for collecting................................ 75
    form of warrant for collection of 77
    overdue may be collected by trustees 76
    non-resident, uncollected, how obtained 26, 27
    testator's estate liable for in executors' and devisees' hands 77
    application for, to be made to council before August 30
    vote of payers of, unnecessary 28
    mandamus for 31
    (*See* SCHOOL TRUSTEES, TOWNSHIP COUNCIL.)
RECONSIDER MOTION, at school meeting 41
REFUSAL to act as trustee (*See* TRUSTEES, PENALTIES)...............
    to account 34
REGISTERS (*See* TEACHERS, SCHOOL TRUSTEES), school trustees to provide 23
REGISTRATION of title to school site 17
REGULATIONS, SCHOOL :
    penalty for non-observanse of................................... 10
RELIGIOUS INSTRUCTION, children to receive such, as parents desire.... 79
    pupils not required to attend................................... 79
    regulations with respect to..................................... 79
    weekly, by clergyman 79
    EXERCISES, opening and closing each day 79
RENTING. (*See* HOUSE.)
REPAIRING school house authorized............................... 16, 19
REPLEVIN (*See* DECISIONS), definition of........................... 51
REPORT. (*See* TRUSTEES, AUDITORS, INSPECTOR.)
"REQUIRED, WHEN NO LONGER," phrase explained....................... 49
RESCIND resolution of former school meetings 44
RESIDENCE, trustees may erect teacher's 19
    township council to raise money for teacher's 27
RESIDENT. (*See* NON-RESIDENTS, SCHOOL RATES.)
    definition of, and non-resident 31
    and non-resident rates... 22
    pupils between five and twenty-one to be admitted to schools 17
    school accommodation for, children 17

ANALYTICAL INDEX. 97

	PAGE.
RESIGNATION of office by trustee provided fo...	7
RESOLUTION (See SCHOOL MEETING.)	
RESPONSIBILITY, PERSONAL. (See PENALTIES, DECISIONS, TRUSTEES, TREASURER.)	
RETIREMENT of school trustees	9
RETIRING TRUSTEE, power of	9
RETURNING OFFICER, duties of, at school elections	39
penalty on, in certain cases	39
RIGHT to vote. (See VOTE.)	
of children to attend school	54
ROLL, assessors and collectors'. (See Collector.)	28
ROMAN CATHOLIC SEPARATE SCHOOLS. (See SEPARATE SCHOOLS.)	
ROOMS, size of school	18
RULES OF ORDER for rural school meetings... 40, 41,	42

SALARIES. (See TEACHERS, INSPECTORS.)
SALE of school site and premises authorized. (See SITE.)

SATURDAY, every, is a holiday	81
SCHOOL, all free	78
must be kept open by trustees	9
who has right to attend	78
additional	23
ARBITRATIONS. (See AWARDS, ARBITRATORS.)	
ASSESSMENT. (See COUNTY AND TOWNSHIP COUNCIL, SCHOOL TRUSTEES.) Special township for school	29
BOOKS. (See BOOKS, TEXT BOOKS.)	
COLLECTORS. (See COLLECTORS.)	
CORPORATION. (See CORPORATION.)	
ELECTIONS. (See ELECTIONS.)	
ELECTORS who are and form of declaration required from	39
EXPENSES, how provided for... 21,	27
how provided for in cities, towns and villages	76
trustees, sole judge of expediency of	35
FEES. (See FEES.)	
FUND, qualified teachers only entitled to	23
may be withheld, unless regulations are complied with	80
what are lawful	35
responsibilities of certain parties for loss of. (See PENALTIES.)	
HOUSE. (See HOUSE, SCHOOL TRUSTEES), decisions respecting.... 19,	195
holidays	81
restrictions on use of	19
care and repair of	19
LIBRARIES. (See LIBRARIES.)	
MEETING, annual, when held and time of day ... 38,	41
electors at, defined	39
chairman at	39

ANALYTICAL INDEX.

SCHOOL MEETING—(Continued).

	PAGE
chairman, duties of	39
secretary duties	39
secretary, duties of	40
power of as to awards	49
first in new school section	40
three trustees to be elected at first	42
trustees, declaration of office	42
order of business and rules to be observed at	42
mode of putting motions and of recording votes at	40
adjournment of annual or special (difference)	41
copy of proceeding of, to be sent to inspector	41
special meeting may rescind resolution of	44
may reconsider motions at	41
what a special meeting can do	44
trustees to present report at annual	42
auditors to be appointed and to report at annual	42
why are and who are not legal voters at	39
declaration required from voters	39
protest at	41
trustees to give public notice of every ordinary	38
mode of calling a special	44
mode of calling when not called by trustees	38
may be called by inspector	38
to select school site	45
place of annual, to be appointed by the trustees, &c	38
penalty of trustees for not calling certain	11
complaints cannot be entertained unless made within *twenty* days	41
penalty for disturbing	80
what school meeting cannot do	44, 51

(*See* AUDITOR, CHAIRMAN, FREE SCHOOLS.)

MONEYS. (*See* PENALTIES, SECRETARY-TREASURER, TRUSTEE.)

NOTICE. (*See* FORM, NOTICE.)

PREMISES. (*See* HOUSE.)

PROPERTY, trustees to acquire and hold	16
vests absolutely in school corporation	16

RATES. (*See* RATES.)

REGISTER. (*See* REGISTERS.)

SECTION AUDITORS.

inspector to decide difference between	43

SECTIONS. (*See* ALTERATION, UNION SECTIONS, TOWNSHIP COUNCIL.)

altered school, who are trustees of	8
liability of original, for its debts	8

SITE. (*See* SITE.)

TAX on parents and guardians unlawful	76

TEACHER. (*See* TEACHER.)

ANALYTICAL INDEX. 99

SCHOOL—(Continued).
  TERMS 81
  TRUSTEES RURAL SCHOOL. (See FORM, PENALTIES. RESPONSIBILITY,
    SCHOOL RATES.)... 5
    definition of a... 43
  DUTIES. (See POWERS.)
    who may and who may not be 6, 43
    legal decisions respecting 9, 11, 21
    election of, in each section, mode of 43, 142
    how office vacated...................................... 7
    who are of altered school sections...................... 8
    duty as to school site....................... 12, 16, 46, 51
    may sell school site when 17
    power to enlarge school site 49
    cannot contract with member of school corporation ... 13, 36
    entitled to notice of action 11, 15, 16
    school house cannot be sold under a judgment against.... 20
    action against in regard to school site 53
    access to assessment roll 77
    in unorganized townships 72
    election of 39, 40, 41, 42, 43
    term of office in rural section........................ 8
    not to hold office of teacher or inspector............ 56
    powers and duties 5, 6, 14, 16, 21, 22, 23, 32, 33, 35, 49
    personal liability of 9
    legal decisions respecting............................. 11
    must take security from secretary-treasurer and collector 36
    must keep school open................................. 36
    power to make contracts 14
    refusal to account 34
    responsibilities of 5
    cannot be compelled to take office after four years' service expired, 37
    power of retiring 9
    penalty for refusing to serve as 7
    must call school meetings 35
    removal of, or non-attendance of three months, vacates office 7
    report to be submitted to annual meeting 42
    must be resident assessed freeholders and householders 6
    may resign 37
    verbal declaration of office...................... 7, 35, 42
    are a school corporation 14
    cannot perform acts of banking........................ 15
    meetings, notice of, to all members of the corporation........... 36
    two cannot act without consulting third 9, 15
    to take possession of and hold school property and keep in repair, 16, 19
    to provide apparatus, books, &c..................... 21, 36

100 ANALYTICAL INDEX.

SCHOOL DUTIES—(*Continued*).

	PAGE.
can sue for trespass	20
to do what they deem expedient with building, renting, &c.	19
must use corporate seal in all official acts	36
contract under corporate seal binding	9, 10
to provide additional schools when required	3
may establish a female school	24
powers and duties respecting school teachers	21
alone can employ teachers	36
may be sued for refusal to give order to teacher	63
to give orders to qualified teachers only	3, 36
may erect teacher's residence	19
to provide for salaries and expenses	21
may levy school rate at any time	76
rate may include costs of, for defending legal but not illegal acts	77
warrant, form of, and signature to	27
to make out roll and collector's warrant	27
mode of collecting school rates from residents and non-residents	27
may apply to municipality or levy rate themselves	19
form or mode of application to township council	27, 30
to make return of rates to municipal clerk	36
to admit to school, residents between 5 and 21, and to maintain school	36
duty in regard to compulsory education	36, 55
duty as to absentees	55
to have fined, or charge fee for, absentee pupils	36
annual report of	42
to visit schools, and for what	22, 36
to provide register and visitors' book, &c.	23, 36
Masters and Servants Act does not apply	63
authority in regard to non-residents	32, 36
are sole judges of expediency of expenditure	35
to prosecute illegal voters at school meetings	35
approval required before master can expel pupil	59
cannot receive school moneys (unless secretary-treasurer)	12
mandamus to	31
dissent of, as to school site	53
to see that authorized text books are used	22, 36
to establish school section libraries and appoint librarians	22
responsibility of, for lost money, &c	34
to prepare and read report for annual meeting	42
contents of annual report	43
to make *half-yearly* report to inspector	23, 36
to make *annual* report to inspector	36
must exercise corporate powers	11, 14, 36
should appoint auditors	3, 3, 36

ANALYTICAL INDEX. 101

PAGE.

SCHOOL DUTIES—(Continued).
    must submit school accounts to auditors 34, 35
    should appoint secretary-treasurer 36
    must account for books, money, &c 34
    summary of the duties of 35
    may borrow money from municipality 27, 28
    must apply to council before August to levy rate 30
    re-election of, lawful 8
    may sue defaulting secretary-treasurer.................... 25
    (See SITES, ARBITRATION, AWARD, &c.)

SEAL. (See CORPORATE SEAL.)

SECRETARY, appointment of, at school meetings, his duties 39
    TREASURER, (See FORM), appointment and duties of 24
    bond of. (See SECURITY.) 25
    must account 25, 34
    responsibility of for lost money, books, &c.................... 34
    liability of.. 25
    penalty on, for refusing to account for moneys or withholding
        books 25
    mode of proceeding against................................ 25
    decisions regarding 25

SECURITY from school collector and secretary-treasurer............. 9
    consequence of neglect of trustees to take from treasurer 9

SERVANT ACT, master and, does not apply to teachers 63
SICKNESS of teacher.. 62
SIGNATURES of trustees to warrant number required................ 77
SITE, necessity of proper title for school 16
    duty of trustees as to purchase of 16, 45, 51
    trustees to hold by any title 16
    registration of 17
    when question of school site comes up for consideration.. 45
    award-making 47
    taking possession of 50
    tender to owner of award for............................... 50
    dissent of trustees as to 53
    is exempt from taxation................................... 21
    size of, defined 18
    when required to be chosen................................ 15
    kind of, to be chosen..................................... 46
    sale or exchange of old 16, 49, 50
    owner of, refusing to sell, remedy 50
    power of trustees to enlarge 49
    privileges of owner of..................................... 50
    not liable to be sold in judgment 20
    may be sold when not required 17

ANALYTICAL INDEX.

PAGE.

SITE—(*Continued*).
    when rural trustees must obtain approval of meeting before changing old, or when school section established 12, 45
    mistake in conveyance of... 53
    mode of selecting or changing by special meeting 49
    county inspector may call meeting for selecting 46
    when rural trustees must consult constituents in selecting 45
    meeting cannot adjourn without action................................ 45
    failure of meeting to appoint arbitrators 46
    where trustees fail to call menting as to............................ 46
    arbitration in, may be superseded before award made 57
    arbitrators must meet to determine.............................. 46, 47
    remedy when parties refuse to appoint arbitrator on.............. 46
    remedy in case arbitrators should refuse to act.................... 46
    arbitration on, when invalid.. 48
    power of arbitrators on 40
    decisions of the Superior Courts in regard to..................... 51
    township council may purchase or dispose of 51
    reservation for school site building 53
    action against trustees in regard to 53
    (*See* ARBITRATION, AWARD.)
SIZE of school site... 18
    of school rooms 18
    of school house to be determined by school trustees.............. 19
SUBPŒNA, corporation cannot be summoned by; its members may...... 15
SUPERANNUATED TEACHERS AND INSPECTORS, provisions as to. 67
    inspectors' and teachers' payments to fund for.................... 67
    municipal councils, public school board, or board of education may aid 67
    amount representative of teacher entitled to 67, 68
    amount teacher retiring 67, 68
    provision as to superannuated teacher resuming his duties......... 68
SURETIES. (*See* SECURITY), when and when not responsible........ 25, 30
SUSPENSION of teachers' certificates by inspectors 71
    of pupils by teachers 58
SWEEPING school house, and fire, trustees to provide for........ 19, 61

TAXATION, school house and site exempt from 21
    school library property exempt from............................... 22
TAXES. (*See* RATES.)
TEACHERS, PUBLIC SCHOOL, (*See* SUPERANNUATED TEACHERS.)
    who are qualified... 56
    powers and duties of.. 57, 59, 60, 66
    legal decisions respecting... 63
    trustees or inspectors cannot be 56
    cannot sue for trespass on school house........................... 20
    assistant and monitor when to be employed....................... 56

TEACHERS—(Continued).

	PAGE.
residence may be erected for	19
form of agreement with	56
not to teach on legal holidays	81
not to use or permit unauthorized text books	78, 79
no deduction can be made from salary of, for legal holidays	66
trustee to employ qualified, only	23, 36
no rate can be imposed for payment of unqualified	63
certain agreements with, invalid	64
qualified, only entitled to school fund	23
decision respecting trustees agreeing to furnish fuel to	63
inspector signing contract with, is a mere approval of it	63
Master and Servant Act does not apply to	63
cannot sue trustees for school fund but for order if so agreed	63
order to be given to qualified only	23, 36
township council may authorize provision for residence of	27
duty as to school library	61
to teach according to law and regulations	59
to keep and give access to school registers	61
to classify pupils	59
distinction between masters and	57
power to suspend pupils	58
power to expel pupils	59
when to be in their schools	60
is bound to fulfil agreement to teach, &c	66
religious teaching	79
institutes	81
associations	82
mandamus for rate for salary	64
enforcement of agreement with trustees	64
proceedings to recover salary	64
duty with regard to school premises	60
absence and sickness of	62, 66
visiting other schools	62
presents, subscriptions, &c., to, forbidden	63
teachers' meetings	63
shall not act as agent for sale of books, &c	80
representation of character of, privileged	64
to maintain order and discipline	58
to give access to registers' and visitors' book	62, 65
consequence to, of refusing to give up school house key, &c	65
to hold public examinations, and give notice	65
form of notice of examination	65
to furnish information to Minister and to inspector	66
to report half-yearly to inspector	23
protection of in regard to salary	66

TEACHERS—*(Continued).*
 cheque must be made payable to 70
 inspector may suspend certificate of 71
 matters of difference with trustees to be decided in division court... 66
TEACHING hours, number of, in a day.. 60
TERM of office by trustees.. 8
 school, length of 81
TESTATOR, executor as well as, liable for rate on non-resident land...... 77
TEXT-BOOKS:
 provisions of the law in regard to 22
 pupils must be furnished with... 22
 trustees and teachers to permit no unauthorized 2, 78, 79
 may be purchased and charged for....................................... 22
TITLE to school property is in trustee corporation......................... 16
 necessity for proper 16
 registration of 16
TOWNSHIP ASSESSOR. (*See* ASSESSOR)
 collector. (*See* COLLECTOR.)
 CLERK, to allow trustees to copy assessor's roll 77
  mandamus to compel, to give trustees access to assessment roll. 77, 35
 COUNCIL 29
  application to... 29
  to pass by-law acquiring and disposing of school property 51
  may purchase site and build school house........................... 51
  raising school moneys... 27, 28, 29
  must levy and collect the sums desired by the trustees 26
  may levy special assessment... 28
  must issue debentures for loan................................. 29, 30
  may raise money for teacher's residence and school purposes....... 27
  may not levy more than one rate in the year in certain cases....... 28
  meeting in August, trustees' application for rate to be made at..... 30
  maximum rate of interest to be paid by 29
 UNORGANIZED. (*See* SECRETARY-TREASURER.)
  orders on, illegal circulation of... 15
  liability of sureties 30
TREES and plants, &c., on school site 18
TRESPASS, suit for, trustee entitled to notice of action 11, 15, 16
 trustees, and not teacher, to sue for, on school house............... 20
TRUSTEE. (*See* SCHOOL TRUSTEE.)

UNORGANIZED TOWNSHIPS, schools in.................................... 72
 formation of school section in 72
 size of school sections in.. 72
 election and powers of trustees in 72
 school assessments in 72
 duty of stipendiary magistrate and inspector in 72

ANALYTICAL INDEX.

UNORGANIZED TOWNSHIPS—(Continued).
    revision of school assessment roll in 72, 73, 74
    appointment and payment of collector 74
    powers of collector 74, 75
    decisions relating to collection of rates 75
UNQUALIFIED TEACHERS, not entitled to school moneys 23
VACANCY in the office of school trustee to be supplied 40
VACATIONS. (See HOLIDAYS.)
VACATE office of rural trustee, how to 7
VERBAL declaration of office by rural trustees 7, 42
VISIT their schools, trustees to 22
    twice a year, public and separate schools, by inspector 69
    teachers may, other schools 62
VISITORS' SCHOOL, trustees must provide teacher a book to keep for 23
VOTE. (See SCHOOL MEETING, ELECTIONS.)
    mode of recording, at school meetings 41
    chairman has casting, and no other 39
    when consent of ratepayers is necessary to rate of loan 28
    right to, at public school meetings 39
    declaration required in case of objection to 39
VOTING, hours of 38
WARMING school house, trustees to provide for 19, 61
WARRANT to trustees of collector to be signed by at least two trustees .. 77
    form of, for the collection of school rate 77
WITNESSES, school section auditors may administer oaths to 34
    when necessary in arbitration cases 34
WOOD. (See FUEL, WARMING.)
WRIT OF MANDAMUS, definition of 77
    township clerk, compelled by, to give trustees access to roll 77
    council may be compelled to collect trustees' estimate, by 81
    to school trustees 31, 64
    municipal corporation 31
    not granted when other remedies can be had 77
    form of 13
WRITING, agreement with teachers must be in, and sealed 56

www.ingramcontent.com/pod-product-compliance
Lightning Source LLC
Chambersburg PA
CBHW020152170426
43199CB00010B/1008